CAGE & AVIARY

CW00324325

COCKATIELS

Other titles available

The Budgerigar Book
by Ernest Howson
Budgerigar Breeding for Beginners
by James Blake
Cult of the Budgerigar
by W Watmough Revised by Cyril Rogers
Inbreeding Budgerigars
by Dr M D S Armour, Revised by Cyril Rogers
World of Budgerigars
by Cyril H Rogers
Homing Budgerigars
by The Duke of Bedford

Parrot-like birds

Speaking Parrots
by Dr. K Russ
Peach Faced Lovebirds (and Related Colours)
by Ian Harman
New Zealand Parrakeets (Kakarikis)
by Dr J Batty

Other cage birds

Breeding British Birds in Aviaries and Cages
by H Norman, Revised by James Blake
Cage Bird Hybrids
by Charles Houlton, Revised by James Blake
World of Zebra Finches
by Cyril Rogers
Mules and Hybrids
by Rosslyn Mannering
The Starlings of Africa
Pam and Dave Bunney

COCKATIELS

Sheila M Thompson

Nimrod Press Limited
15 The Maltings
Turk Street
Alton, Hants GU34 1DL

First published in 1990

Limp Edition ISBN 1-85259-140-4
Cased Edition ISBN 1-85259-144-7

Published by
Nimrod Press Limited
15 The Maltings
Turk Street
Alton, Hants GU34 1DL

Produced by
Jamesway Graphics
18 Hanson Close
Middleton
Manchester M24 2HD

Printed in England

CONTENTS

ACKNOWLEDGEMENTS

I would like to thank Mr Ray Baxter for all his help, kindness and understanding.

A special thank you to my husband Roger for devoting all his spare time to building the avaries.

I would also like to thank Tony and Kevin Clarke for allowing my husband to photograph their white faced cockatiels.

COCKATIELS

PREFACE

The reason I have written this book is that when I bought Kim, my pet cockatiel and the first cockatiel that I had ever owned, I had difficulty in obtaining English books about cockies, as they are affectionately called. There were quite a few American books available but most of the articles and medications mentioned were not obtainable in this country. The unavailability of English books made me decide to write one myself sometime in the future, when I had gained more experience, in the hope that it will help others.

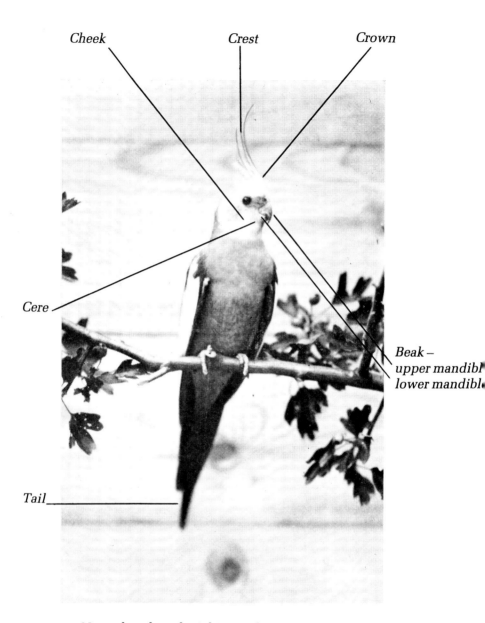

Cheek

Crest

Crown

Cere

Beak –
upper mandibl
lower mandibl

Tail

Normal cock cockatiel (Nymphicus hollandicus)

CHAPTER 1

THE FAMILY PET

Cockatiels which are pretty, friendly birds related to the Cockatoo, originate from Australia, where they are also known as Quarrion or Top Knot Parrakeets. They lead a rather nomadic life and can be found near water sites travelling in pairs and flocks. Although wild, they are not really a timid bird and will venture sometimes into gardens and parks. They feed on grasses, berries, seeds, fruit, grain and the farmers crops. They spend a lot of time on the ground and occasionally, grubs and insects are also eaten. Being hardy birds, they have a fairly long life span of up to twenty to twenty five years.

NORMAL COLOUR

In its wild state, the normal colouring of the cockatiel is mainly grey but of various shades with a striking border of white on the lower edge of its folded wings. It is a long slender bird approximately twelve inches long, half of its length being a long tapering tail. The upper tail feathers of the cock bird are a silvery grey with black colouring underneath, the hen bird having striped yellow bars on the underside of hers. She also has pale yellow polka dots on her long flight feathers which can only be seen when she spreads her wings. Both male and female birds have a high crest, approximately one and a half inches long on top of their heads, which they can raise or lower at will, depending on their mood. The adult cock bird has a bright yellow face and his crest is a mixture of bright yellow and grey feathers, whereas the adult hen bird has only a small amount of yellow on her face and her crest is mainly grey. Both birds have orange-red cheek or ear patches, the males being a lot brighter in colour. He also has some white colouring at the sides of his crown but the hen does not Their feet which have two toes at the front and two at the back are perfect for climbing and are various shades of grey. Their hooked beaks are also grey but their eyes can be either black or brown.

BABY BIRDS

The baby birds of both sexes resemble adult females until they are approximately six months old. It is then that the male bird begins to show more of the yellow colouring on his face and the feathers on the underside of his tail begin to turn black. He also begins to lose the polka dots on his flight feathers and his cheek patches get brighter in colour. At the age of twelve months he has full adult colouring.

Charlie at three and a half weeks old

SEXING

It is for this reason that most people find it difficult to sex a Cockatiel before it is six months of age. In my experiences young males can be told before this time by their whistle or song. Some hens attempt to whistle and can sometimes fool you but on the whole they are a much quieter bird.

When I bought my pet bird Kim, it was thought at the time by the breeder who sold her to me that she was a cock bird. However time proved him to be wrong and when her face did not turn yellow, I knew I had a hen. The breeder did offer to exchange her or give me my money back but by that time I had become so attached to her, I could not part with her.

Since I have had an aviary of my own, I pride myself on having 90 per cent success in determining the sex of the chicks, bred by my birds, within a few weeks of them being fully feathered and out of the nestbox.

DELIGHTS OF COCKATIELS

Until you own one yourself, you will never know what a delightful pet and good company, a cockatiel can be. The affection between a cockie and its owner has to be seen to be believed. They are, in my opinion, the most intelligent, charming and affectionate birds in the world. They are amongst the most popular of the parrot-like birds, as well as their friendliness they are easy to feed and not too expensive to buy.

Along with the budgerigar, a cockatiel is one of the easiest birds in the world to tame. A bird purchased between the ages of ten to sixteen weeks is best and can be tamed regardless of its sex, in a very short time, although I find that hens are more easily tamed than cock birds. Some cockatiels become so tame they will go to anyone, however, although Kim is very tame and affectionate with my husband and myself, she is not keen on strangers. If anyone else puts their hand up to her she tends to fly away. She loves both of us to rub our noses around the sides and back of her head, to her its sheer bliss. She will let me stroke her down her throat with my finger but it does depend on the mood she is in. She is not very keen on fingers in general but I can do what I like to her with my nose. Most cockies love to have the backs of their heads scratched or stroked but not Kim. She is also funny about things on peoples heads, she doesn't like hats or head scarves. Although I have had her for over nine years now, she still gets upset when I wash my hair and wrap a towel round my head. She hisses at me and flies round the room like a wild thing. As soon as I remove the towel she is all right again and flies onto my shoulder.

TEACHING COCKATIELS TO TALK
If you want your bird to talk, it should be kept by itself. However, once it has learnt to talk, another younger bird can be put with it and the older bird should teach the younger one to talk. A cockatiels voice is not raucous like some parrots. It is melodious, clearer than a budgerigars but it is still fairly high pitched. Both male and female cockatiels have been known to talk, the male perhaps better than the female as hens tend to be more temperamental. Cockies can also whistle and imitate tunes. I would like to point out that Kim has never spoken a word in her life, yet a neighbour has a hen that talks very well. It may be that she has spent a lot more time with her bird but I go out to work. I have been told that hand-reared cockatiels are more likely to talk than ones raised by their natural parents in an outside aviary. The reason being the baby birds consider themselves to be tiny human beings and try and copy their foster parents. When teaching a bird to talk, only let one member of the family teach the bird at first as different voice tones can confuse the bird. A woman is probably the best teacher as her voice is more high pitched than a mans. Either let one person do all the teaching or each member of the family teach a different word or phrase. You can also try taping your voice saying for example, 'Hello Peter', over and over again and then playing the tape back to the bird, two or three times a day. More if you can stand it.

BUY FROM REPUTABLE SOURCE
When you obtain your bird, buy him from a reputable dealer and make sure that the bird is healthy. He should be alert and interested in what is going on around him. His eyes should be bright and clear, the nose or cere should be clean with no discharge and his feathers should be smooth with no bald patches. However, do not worry if the bird has one or two feathers missing for example, on its wings or tail as flying around in cages that are too small and being handled can damage the plumage. Check that the feathers around the vent are not dirty because this is a sign of diarrhoea which can be difficult to cure. If possible, check that the bird has good weight by feeling his chest and if his breastbone protrudes do not buy him. His droppings should be firm, the matter being black and white, black being the faeces and the white, urine. The birds breathing should be steady and even.

SETTLING IN

After getting the bird home leave it alone for a few hours to settle down and explore its new home. If possible, buy the bird early in the day so it has time to get used to its new surroundings before nightfall. If you cannot do this and have to collect it in the evening, do not leave it in the dark but give it enough light to adjust to its surroundings. A night light for example like you would leave burning in a child's bedroom is ideal, otherwise it might flutter about and bump into the perches etc, injuring itself. Don't leave it in too bright a light or it will not be able to rest properly. The bird should settle down after a few days.

Do not worry if it does not eat for the first twenty four hours as the bird may be a little homesick at first and miss the other birds in the aviary or shop from where it came. If he does not start eating after a couple of days, check his droppings. If they are bright green, brown, loose or watery, seek professional advice at once. If his droppings are normal and the bird appears healthy, he may not be eating because he's not used to feeding from seed pots or the ones in his cage differ from the ones he's been used to. If this is the case it will take him a little while to get used to the new pots and in the meantime he could starve to death. It has been known to happen. Try scattering some seed on the floor of the cage and see if he eats this. If he does, see that there is seed scattered in this way until he adjusts to his new lifestyle and starts using the pots. You can then gradually stop scattering the seed. Also hang a millet spray up by the perch on which he sits and see if he feeds on this. Please note that a cockatiel needs open pots to feed from and not tubelike feeders that are suitable for smaller kinds of birds.

USING CAGES

A canary or budgerigar cage is not large enough for a cockatiel as a cockie needs plenty of room for his long beautiful tail, he does not like to catch it on anything. The cage should be made of metal and no smaller than two feet long by two feet high and a foot wide (the larger the better) and should have horizontal wires or bars on at least two sides, preferably the front and back. A typical parrot cage that has vertical bars all around it is no good at all, as cockies like to climb and cannot do so if there are no horizontal bars. They have been known to slip and hang themselves by trying to climb vertical bars. The door should be large enough to get your hand through with the bird on it, without touching anywhere as birds are sometimes nervous about moving through small openings. A cage door that is hinged at the bottom is the most convenient as the door then serves as a landing stage for your pet. Please note that the cage size mentioned above applies if you only want one bird. If you want two birds then you must have a larger cage.

Most cages are sold with plastic perches which are not good for the birds feet, so if the cage you buy has this type of perch, I would suggest that you change them for wooden ones. The best perch is three quarters of an inch dowelling or natural wood, bearing in mind that natural wood will need replacing as the bird will gradually gnaw it away. If possible, have a variety of diameters ranging from five eights of an inch (no smaller) up to broom handle size, so your pet can have a change of grip.

It is most important that you do not site the cage in a draught or in direct sunlight. Neither should it be put in a cold place, or where there are fumes of any kind (fumes from non-stick frying pans are especially harmful), high up near a ceiling or in front of a window. A

A cage with horizontal bars

draught can kill a bird. It can cause colds, asthma, pneumonia and kidney troubles. Overheating or too much sun is just as harmful. The back of the cage should where possible, be placed against a wall to give your pet a feeling of security but it should be kept well away from radiators as the dry heat can be damaging to your pets health, the continual moult that can result saps the strength of the bird. You should not place the cage close to or on top of the television, near a radio or telephone etc as loud noises can make the bird nervous. Neither should it be kept in the kitchen where there are fumes from stoves or gas cookers, cooking food and fats. The temperature changes that occur in a kitchen can also make a bird ill.

It is essential that the cage is cleaned out regularly. If the bird is allowed out a lot like mine is, then once a week will probably be sufficient but if the bird is caged up a great deal, then two or three times a week may be necessary particularly if the bird is moulting. You will have to use your own discretion.

The food and water containers should be washed with soap and water at least once a week and each time the bird makes a mess in or on them. Metal containers should not be used because of corrosion and cleaning difficulties.

The perches will probably need to be cleaned every now and then, especially when they are soiled with either food or faeces. Clean them with coarse not smooth sandpaper or a perch scrapper obtainable from pet shops. Never let your bird sit on a wet perch as this can lead to colds and arthritic problems. If you must wash them, make sure that they are completely dry before replacing them in the cage. Washed sand can be used as a cage bottom covering and renewed each time the cage is cleaned. It helps for easier cleaning and is also beneficial to your pet as sand contains calcium and other minerals.

The cage can be covered at night but this is not at all necessary. If you do decide to cover the cage, it must be done every night without fail. The bird, having further insulation provided by the cover, will lose a layer of its downy feathers to compensate and if the cover is left off one night, the bird could easily catch cold. If you have been in the practice of covering the cage at night and want to discontinue doing so, it is best done during the summer months when the weather is warmer. When your pet has his next moult, he will grow a heavier layer of feathers for future insulation.

FOOD AND DRINK

A cockie should be given best canary seed, parrakeet mixture and millet sprays to eat. If you do not buy him parrakeet mixture, then he

This hopper will hold enough seed for a number of birds
(Courtesy: Haines Aviary economy)

will also need some sunflower seeds. I have found that some cockatiel owners are in the habit of feeding their birds on sunflower seeds
alone. This is totally wrong. The birds can become very overweight.
They need a varied diet which gives them much needed vitamins
and minerals to keep them in tip top condition. If preferred, you can
make your own parrakeet mixture using red and white millets,
hemp, buckwheat, clipped oats and sunflower seeds. I mix seven
pounds of mixed millets to three pounds of sunflower seeds, one
pound clipped oats, one pound buck wheat and half a pound hemp.

A piece of cuttlefish and a mineral or iodine block should be hung
up in the cage. The cuttlefish helps to keep the birds beak in trim and
contains both salt and calcium. It is most essential that grit is given
(fine oystershell and mineralised tonic grit are the two I use), as grit
is your birds teeth and helps him to digest his seed. A quarter of a
pound of each mixed together and given in a small pot will last for
months. A honey bar given as a treat will be greatly appreciated by
your pet. The layer of husks that lie on top of your birds seed should

 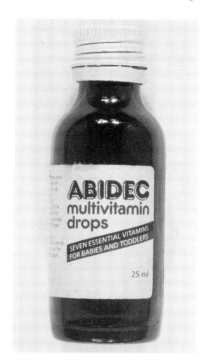

Other essentials: a) cuttlefish bone   b) vitamins
Cuttlefish bone may be bought by weight or in a packet as above

be removed daily as birds cannot find the seed under a thick layer of husks and may starve. I blow them off onto the garden and let the wild birds have a picking.

Fresh water should be given daily and two or three times a week a vitamin supplement should be added to it. I use Abidec, which is obtainable from chemists and is usually given to human babies. It is rather expensive to buy but it does last a long time However, most pet shops sell cheaper products. Once a month, the bird can be given a *tiny* pinch of Bicarbonate of Soda in its drinking water, which is brought to the boil and cooled. This helps to clean out the birds system and sweetens the crop. A vitamin supplement such as PYM should be sprinkled on to the seed on a regular basis and a few drops of Vitapet conditioning oil can be mixed with the seed (just enough to make it tacky) once or twice a week. This gives them vitamins A, B, D and E. Both these products are obtainable from pet stores.

Fresh greens should be given daily when available. They can be dandelions, turnip tops, celery, spinach, chicory, endive, Brussel

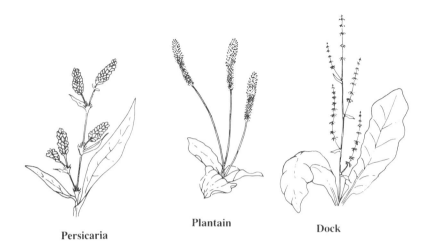

Persicaria

Plantain

Dock

Chickweed

Green food is essential

sprouts, cabbage, carrot tops and watercress. Lettuce can also be
given but this does not have a lot of food value. In summer, grasses
such as chickweed and shepherds purse are greatly enjoyed. Please
make sure that all green food and grasses are thoroughly washed
before being given to your bird. After being well washed in
lukewarm water they should be dried with a towel. Never feed
greens straight from the fridge as they will be too cold.

Some birds enjoy a piece of carrot or an apple, banana or orange. If

Pots I use for seed and grit

your bird does not accept the greens or fruit immediately, do not stop supplying them as he has to acquire a taste for new foods. If he will not eat whole pieces of carrot or apple, try grating or chopping them up very finely. This can make all the difference. All greens and fruit should be removed from the cage before they become stale and mouldy.

Do not feed your pet on white bread, cakes, fat or sugar. However, a limited amount of sweet biscuit may be given. Do not over do it or your pet may become too fat.

Fresh branches and twigs are nourishing as well as being greatly appreciated. Cockatiels are greedy chewers and will spend hours gnawing the bark off. The trees which can be used for this purpose are alder, hazelnut, elm, sloe, hawthorn, willow, flowering cherries, citrus and other fruit trees. All branches and twigs should be thoroughly washed before being given to your bird. I think it is common knowledge, that on no account should branches and twigs be used off a laburnum tree as it is highly poisonous, the bark on oak, maple, sycamore and lilac is also poisonous and therefore these trees should not be used.

TAMING YOUR COCKATIEL

Once the bird becomes thoroughly accustomed to its new home, usually eight to ten days, then the owner can begin taming. If the bird is unusually nervous, leave him for a few weeks until he settles down before you try to tame him. Start the training by opening the door of the cage and very slowly offer a piece of millet to the bird. Hold it steady while the bird eats, then withdraw your hand and close the cage door. Repeat this several times until the bird is eating from your hand without any signs of nervousness. The next step is to try to gradually ease one of your fingers under the birds feet so it is sitting on that finger while it is eating out of your other hand. Do this several times. Once you think the bird is sitting on your finger without any fear whatsoever, slowly draw your hand to the cage door, out into the room and back into the cage again. Repeat this several times. After a while, leave the cage door open and let the bird come out and have a fly around the room, but before doing so, close all windows and doors, cover up any mirrors and draw your curtains until the bird gets used to the room, otherwise your pet may fly into the glass injuring itself. Introduce the bird to the glass by letting him flutter against it. Cockatiels are marvellous flyers, in fact one of the fastest of all Australian parrakeets and like to exercise their wings daily. Never leave doors and windows open anywhere in the house when your bird is at liberty. After he becomes tame and full of confidence, he will want to explore especially if you are in a different room to him and he will try and find you.

A caged bird that is not allowed out of its cage will become fat, dull and bored through having little exercise and plenty to eat and will not usually live as long as a bird that is allowed out and getting plenty of exercise. Flying keeps the wings and muscles firm, prevents the bird from getting fat and he will be a far healthier and happier pet. The bird will usually go back into its cage of its own accord, especially when it is hungry but one of the advantages of a tame bird is that it can be put back into its cage whenever the owner chooses and not when the bird decides.

If when you try and tame him you have difficulty in getting a finger under the birds feet, try to get him to step onto your hand instead. Offer a piece of millet to him by holding it between your thumb and first finger in such a way that the millet lies across the back of your hand. Over a period of days, offer the millet between the other fingers, keeping your hand flat with the palm downwards. Each time the millet is offered in this way it will be farther away from the bird and eventually he will have to step onto your hand in order to reach it. Do not jerk your hand away if he goes to peck at it. The bird is only testing your reaction and if you pull away he will think he has got the better of you.

Try stroking the birds tummy several times a day, pressing slightly harder each time (but not so hard as to knock him off the perch) and one day, hopefully he will step off the perch onto your finger.

All doors and windows must be kept closed while the bird is out of its cage, all green plants and flowers should be removed from the room and gas and electric fires should have guards around them. Green plants attract the bird and if eaten can cause trouble with the birds digestion. You will find that your pet will spend a lot of time running about on the floor, so please be very careful that you do not tread on him. I know of several people who have lost cockies because of a few moments carelessness.

Some cockatiels become 'one man' birds. This is usually because one member of the family pays more attention to him than the others do and therefore this person becomes his favourite. To avoid this happening, let all the members of the family share in the tasks of feeding, cleaning the cage and handling the bird.

If he bites you it is because he is nervous or frightened. Never hit him but say 'NO' very loudly if he does go to bite and offer him some millet to distract him. If he hisses at you, it is because you have disturbed him either when he is resting, eating or preening. He will also hiss at a stranger. It is a normal reaction from your pet so please do not reprimand him for it.

A cockatiel does not play with toys in the same way that a budgerigar does, instead he likes to chew things but he will appreciate a bell in his cage as well as a few twigs to gnaw. You can also give him a mirror. A cockatiel does not like to be left alone for long periods and if this happens, the bird can suffer from loneliness and boredom. If you cannot spend sufficient time with your pet then providing it with a mirror will at least give it some comfort. Some people will tell you that providing a bird with a mirror stops him from learning to talk but I have never found this to be so. A neighbour of mine has a budgerigar and I have never heard a budgie talk like he does and he has a mirror. I also know of several cockatiels that talk and they all have mirrors.

You will find that once you let your pet loose into the room, he will find his own playground and playthings, On my dining room table, I have a glass bowl set inside a wooden surround. The glass bowl has fluted edges so there are small gaps between these edges and the wooden surround. Kim likes to chew up bits of paper and

A bird bath is essential

drops the tiny pieces down the gaps. She also likes playing with a shoelace and will spend hours with one chewing the ends. It looks like a dummy in her beak. Roger, my husband, made a swing for her out of a wire coat hanger and a piece of dowelling. It hangs from the curtain rail and Kim sits on it looking out of the window. It also acts as a landing stage for her when she flies around the room.

You could also try making a playpen for your bird. It needn't be anything elaborate. A tray to catch any droppings, a Y shaped branch attached to it, to which is hung a shoelace, a bell, a piece of string etc, a ladder to climb, will give hours of pleasure. However, do not leave the bird unattended while he is playing with string or a shoe-lace as he could come to grief, he could hang himself. I have never known it to happen but there is always a first time.

Don't think your pet will never fly away so be very careful as you go through doors. If he does escape outside into the garden, do not panic and chase him. If he remains in the garden, stay calm, get a net and try and catch him. If this fails, try placing his cage outside, complete with seed and water, where he can see it. Hopefully, he will return to it when he is hungry. If you have another cockatiel, place his cage next to the open one outside and the calling of this bird may encourage the other one to come back. If he flies away and disappears from sight, all you can do then is advertise for his return.

BATHING

A cockatiel in the wild takes a bath in the rain. He spreads his wings looking like a big butterfly, letting the rain fall down on him, trying to catch every drop. A pet bird will appreciate a bath but he will have to be encouraged to take a bath in a large, flat dish or bowl, preferably shallow, although Kim flies into the kitchen when I am at the sink and I have to put *two inches of warm water,* not hot, in the washing up bowl for her to bath in. As an alternative, you can spray warm water over your bird with a fine mist sprayer. However, some birds do not like to be sprayed. Kim doesn't. You can buy commercial sprays from a pet shop but these usually have an oil base to put a shine on the feathers. These sprays should never be used on a cockatiel because of the powdery nature of its feathers.

MATTERS TO WATCH

If your bird opens his mouth, stretches and crooks his neck, he is not choking or trying to swallow something. He is either exercising his throat muscles, (which can last from a few seconds to several minutes), or if he continues to do it for an hour or more, does not seem able to stop and seems distressed, then it may be digestion trouble.

This happened a couple of times to Kim. The first time it happened I had not had her very long and did not know much about birds at the time. I kept letting her have titbits which I now know was entirely wrong. The first time she started 'gaping' as I call it, I had let her peck at a bun I was eating and apparently she could not digest it. She started gaping, could not stop and seemed distressed so I tried massaging her crop with my finger. She then started to vomit and eventually brought up a lump of dough. After this she was all right again.

The second time she gaped for over three hours, wanted to sleep and could not. She had not been eating our food this time. I tried massaging her crop but this time it did not work so I had to try something else. I mixed a few grains of Bicarbonate of Soda with a tablespoon of water, filled an eye-dropper with the solution and with Rogers help emptied a few drops into her beak. This seemed to help her and after a short while she stopped gaping.

Overgrown claws
should be trimmed
by snipping off
the excess growth
below the vein, which
runs part of the way
down the nail

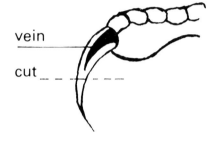

Cutting claws

CUTTING CLAWS

Occasionally, you may find that your pets claws have become over-grown and when this happens, they will need filing or clipping. If you clip them you must be very careful not to cut the vein. If you hold the claw up to the light you should be able to see where the vein begins. Using nail clippers or sharp scissors just take off the tip of the claw, one eighth of an inch is plenty, as you can always take more off. If you do happen to catch the vein, dip the claw in Witch Hazel, Alum or Friars Balsam to stop the bleeding. You may have to hold the claw for a few seconds until the blood congeals. If you do not like the idea of clipping the claws then try filing them but it will take longer to do. You should always file any rough edges from the claws otherwise they may catch on your clothes or other material and this could injure your bird when he goes to fly away.

On very rare occasions the birds beak may become overgrown but if he is regularly provided with plenty of chewing material, this should not happen. If it does, then the beak must be trimmed by a veterinary surgeon.

If your pet does a 'whoopsy' when out of its cage, the dropping can be removed straight away with a tissue or left to dry and then brushed off.

There are just two more things I would like to mention that you will experience when acquiring a cockatiel as a pet. First of all, a cockie goes through a baby stage like a kitten or a puppy. (Kim used to peck the lampshades). Please do not confine the bird in its cage and vow never to let it out again. It is only a passing phase and should stop as the bird grows older. Just make sure that the bird is not left to its own devices in a room by itself. Make sure that someone is there with the bird, so that if it goes to peck at anything it should not, it can be stopped. If possible, remove the article out of its reach for the time being. Be especially careful where there are electric wires. If the bird should peck them, he could be electrocuted.

Secondly, a bird has its baby moult around five months of age and because it also has to adjust to the temperature of your home, it will lose a lot of its downy feathers which it needed for insulation when it was housed outside. Therefore, it will have a heavy moult for a few weeks but once this initial moult has finished, further moults should never be quite as bad again.

I will finish this first chapter with a few more words about Kim. She has found a new toy. Roger keeps his loose change in a little dish on the wall unit. Kim gets inside this dish and throws the coins out all over the place. The only trouble is that she doesn't put them back again, she leaves that for us to do. The wall unit also has some ornaments on the top shelf. Kim sits on this shelf and gets hold of the animal ornaments (two cats and a dog) by the ears or tail and turns them right round so that they are facing the wall. I do not think she likes them looking at her.

CHAPTER 2

THE AVIARY

BUILDING MATERIALS

An aviary can be built of various materials including wood, brick and cement but whatever is used, the shelter must be well made, have plenty of ventilation but be free from draughts. It should not be sited anywhere near noisy places such as a busy road, a dustbin or where passers by will continually disturb the birds. Choose a site that you think your birds will enjoy the most and benefit from. A place where they can receive all the fresh air they need, have sufficient light and be protected from the elements of bad weather.

There are books available on building aviaries, but I will describe mine in case it is of interest to the reader. It was originally built with the colony breeding system in mind but after having several problems during the first breeding season (which I will describe to you in a later chapter) it was redesigned.

OUR EXPERIENCES

We bought a good quality shed, made to order, the size being seven feet long by five feet wide and seven feet six inches to the eaves. It is of the lean to type but this is not important. However, a shed with an apex roof would probably cost you more.

Thinking ahead to the cold weather, Roger, my husband, insulated the shed or shelter (ceiling, walls, roof, door and floor) with five eighths inch insulation board (fibreboard) and covered this with hardboard. As well as insulating, the hardboard stops the birds from pecking the fibreboard. Although cockatiels are very hardy birds and

An attractive aviary is essential

Adequate perching

Covered shelter

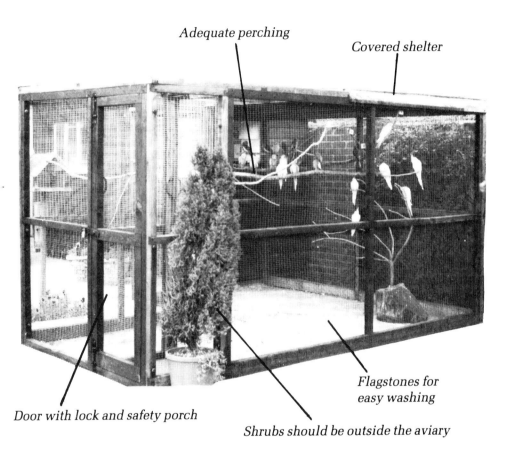

Flagstones for
easy washing

Door with lock and safety porch

Shrubs should be outside the aviary

do not require any heat during the winter months, it is essential that they are protected from draughts and their feet protected from frost. By insulating the shelter it ensured that even when the weather was bitterly cold, the birds could rest in a dry and draught proof environment without any harm befalling them. Many varieties of birds do not mind the cold weather provided it is a dry- and not a wet-cold.

The shed window, which measured three and a half feet by two and a half feet, was covered on the inside with wire netting. Birds cannot see glass, they fly into it headfirst and can do themselves a lot of harm, therefore all glass used in an aviary should be covered with wire netting.

Beneath the window, a wooden shelf was fastened for the seed, grit and waterpots to stand on. The pots should be good and solid, made of earthenware, pottery or strong plastic, that will stand firmly on the shelf and not get knocked off. I use plastic ones myself. They should be placed within easy reach of both the birds and the breeder. Millet sprays, cuttlefish and mineral or iodine blocks can be hung up on the wire netting and the birds will then climb up and peck at them.

An inner door was made from sixteen gauge wire, one inch by a half inch, set in a light wooden frame and fitted with a lock and a bolt. This inner door, or safety door, is necessary when entering the shelter from the outside as you are entering blind and cannot see where your birds are. You can fasten the outside door behind you before opening the inner one and so prevent the birds from escaping. Cockatiels are great escape artists.

The floor must be made secure against any intrusion of vermin. Mice and rats can be a nuisance for they disturb nesting birds and foul the seed and water, which can cause a health problem, so close, heavy wooden boards were used. As previously stated, insulation board was laid on top of this and then covered with hardboard. You can use concrete or stone slabs as an alternative. A thoroughly dry floor in the shelter is most important to the birds' health in both summer and winter, so ours is covered by wood shavings which are renewed periodically when soiled. Newspaper could be used instead of shavings but this would have to be renewed each day.

An opening or bobhole was made in the side of the shed for the birds' entry into the flight. To deflect any draught entering the shelter by way of the bobhole when it is open, two pieces of wood were fitted at an angle, one on the inside of the bobhole and one on the outside.

PERCHES

Perches of various diameters were made from five eighths and three quarters of an inch dowelling, broom handles and natural tree branches that the birds could gnaw. They were fitted at different places in the shelter but not directly above the seed and water pots, otherwise the birds' droppings would constantly foul them. The perches should vary in thickness so that the birds can have a change of grip and their feet will not become cramped by having to sit on perches all the same size. All perches should be firmly fixed, as insecure perches can prevent the birds from mating properly and this can result in infertile eggs.

Cockatiels like roosting at night in crannies or holes, the higher the better, so if you can make some provision for this I am sure the birds will appreciate it. My birds like a shelf that Roger put up all along the one side of the shelter. He fixed it fairly high up and, with small pieces of wood, divided it into partitions. Each partition is large enough to accommodate two pairs of birds. Do not make the holes or crannies too large or the birds may mistake them for nesting boxes and try to lay their eggs in them.

The whole interior of the shelter was painted with white emulsion paint and the exterior was painted with Cuprinol.

LIGHTING

An electric light operated by a dimmer switch is invaluable in the shelter. It can be used as a night light at nesting time and to extend feeding periods when necessary. It can be used to settle the birds down in the evening and to settle in new arrivals. Another time that I use it is on bonfire night. If the birds are startled by any fireworks and come off their perches, they can see where they are if the light is on low and can fly back to their perches without any injuries being sustained. Birds should not be plunged from bright light into total darkness as the shock can cause them to panic and leave their roosting places. If they crash into the aviary walls or roof, they can injure themselves, sometimes fatally. Any electric light bulbs inside the shelter must be protected by a wire screen or similar object so that the birds cannot come into contact with them.

THE SHELTER

Some breeders send their birds into the shelter at night and I am in full agreement with this. My friend Ray tells me I worry too much but I am always afraid that if the birds are allowed to sleep outside during the night, cats may disturb them and if they are disturbed,

Aviary with shelter

they cannot always find their way back to their roosting places in the dark. They could injure themselves trying. Also if the weather becomes worse during the night, ie rain, frost, snow, or there is a severe drop in temperature, the birds could catch cold or even die. If there is a frost and the birds are roosting, clinging to the wire netting, like some of them do, their feet could freeze to the wire and they would be unable to move.

They would probably be all right during the warmer months of the year weatherwise but there is still the danger of cats. I have hedgehogs in my garden during the night and these too could frighten the birds. There is also a danger of foxes where I live, one has been seen in my next door neighbour's garden late at night. My birds more often than not go into the shelter of their own accord when the light begins to fade in the evenings. There have been a few occasions when they decided they wanted a night out and I have had to send them in, but on the whole they are very good.

Roger made a sliding wooden door that fits over the bobhole, or pophole as some people call it, and this is operated by a piece of wire

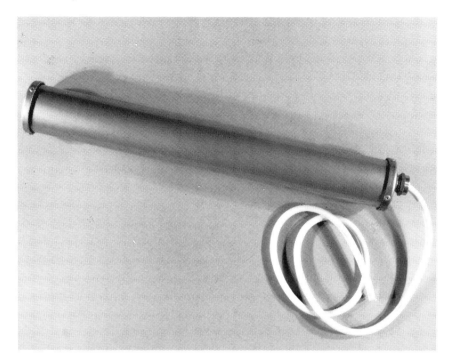

A tubular heater for cold winters

(again from a clothes hanger) which is accessible from outside the aviary.

You will probably find that during the first few days, new birds have to be driven into the shelter at night until they become accustomed to their new surroundings. Birds do not like going into dark places so it is important that the shelter is light enough to attract them.

HEAT AND VENTILATION

On hot summer days there should be plenty of ventilation in the shelter especially when all the birds are shut up together, but here again I must remind you to beware of draughts, as these are more dangerous to the birds than winds.

If warmth is supplied to the birds in winter, it should not exceed 50 degrees F. This can be achieved by either thermostatically controlled heaters, hot water pipes or radiators. Do not use open gas fires or oil fired stoves as these are all dangerous for reasons of poisonous fumes, dirt and the risk of fire. Whatever source of heating is used, it must be kept well away from the birds so they cannot come into contact with it and get burnt. It is important that any birds kept in a heated environment should have plenty of fresh air, (again no draughts) otherwise the dry air, lacking in humidity, causes the feathers to become dry and brittle, the plumage loses its shine and the birds themselves become dull and lifeless.

You can supply humidity by placing a pan of boiling water in some part of the aviary, where the birds will not come into contact with it and letting it evaporate slowly. This process will have to be repeated each time the water has evaporated and this is of course, time consuming.

Up until twelve months ago, my birds have had no form of heating whatsoever and four years ago came through one of the worst winters that I can remember. It was the coldest weather they had ever experienced. The temperature went down to minus 16 degrees F. where we live, (in other places it went even lower) and it went on for such a long time. The water was frozen solid in the drinking pots inside the shelter every morning. Even the droppings were frozen where the birds were roosting but the birds themselves were all right, in fact I had never seen them look healthier. I admit they did not look very happy, they sat all huddled up, but cold, frosty weather is one of nature's ways of controlling disease and a cold spell can be very beneficial to your birds as long as they are kept dry.

However, in case we ever experience another winter as severe as the one previously mentioned, Roger has installed a single tubular heater and by having a separate thermostat, the temperature can be kept at approximately 40 degrees F. This is just to keep the frost at bay and prevent the drinking water from freezing up. Each morning I shall check the temperature, switch the heater off and leave the birds shut up inside until the inside temperature drops to somewhere near the outside temperature. The birds can then be let out into the flight and by doing it this way they should not catch cold.

Although the birds have their own insulation against the cold, I do not think it is advisable to let them out into the flight straight from a heated shelter in bitterly cold weather as they could quite easily catch cold. You will have to decide whether to heat the shelter at a higher temperature and confine the birds to it until the weather gets warmer, or not to heat it at all and let the birds go out into the flight whenever they want, bearing in mind that they must be shut up in the shelter at night, or install a heater like mine and follow my example.

THE FLIGHT

The aviary and flight should be built with the flight being twice the length of the sleeping quarters where possible but this will depend of course on how much space you have available. The more room you give your birds, the healthier and happier they will be.

In constructing our flight, the timber used was a soft wood, treated with a good wood preservative. The construction was relatively simple, making separate frames that were covered with good quality twilweld (sixteen gauge, one half inch by one inch). To make the frames suitably strong, the timber used was of two inch by two inch sections. In exposed places it may be preferable to board up one or even two sides of the flight to protect the birds from severe winds.

You should also bear in mind the threat of predators. We used two foot by two foot slabs for the floor of our flight which also makes it easier to keep clean. As an alternative the wire netting can be buried at least two feet below the ground and turned outwards. If broken glass is placed all around the bottom of the netting, this will give added protection, as rats do not like broken glass. A watch should also be kept on the woodwork of both the shelter and flight so that it is not attacked by mice and rats. If one has started to make a hole, it will not be long before it breaks through with serious consequences.

SAFETY DOORS

At the time, only one door into the flight was considered to be necessary as it was easy to see where the birds were before opening the door and cockatiels are not flappy like some birds are. However, after twelve months, my cockies became so used to me, in fact some became quite tame, that whenever I entered the flight, they flew to meet me. On several occasions, Mandy and Guy settled on my head or shoulder and would not get off when I wanted to leave, so it was decided to make a safety door. Roger extended the flight by another six feet, changing the design to an L-shape and added a safety door.

PERCHES

Natural perches of different thicknesses from flowering cherry trees and willow were used throughout the flight. This type of perching needs to be renewed from time to time but the birds have the advantage of being able to gnaw on it, thus keeping their beaks in trim and reducing boredom. Do not place the perches directly above one another, otherwise the birds on the top perch will soil the birds sitting below them, with their droppings. A swing made from a broom handle and a wire coat hanger was also hung up in the flight.

Wendy and James on a round perch

The birds like to sit in the early morning sunshine so the flight was sited in such a way that it receives the full benefit of the morning sunlight. It was shaded from the mid-day sun by a shade-giving almond tree but the tree became unsafe and had to be chopped down, so we decided to cover part of the flight. Do not cover the top completely; in the summertime, it is important for the birds to have direct sunshine on them for part of the day, (a natural source of Vitamin D) and to be able to let the rain fall onto their feathers. There are not many birds who will sit out in a downpour and if the weather is warm, they will not want to sit in the shelter, so part of the flight next to the shelter was roofed over. It was covered with clear plastic sheeting. Covered in this way, it keeps the perches dry and enables the birds to sit outside if they want to, no matter what the weather. The plastic sheeting is fitted over the top of the wire netting but be careful that the birds cannot peck at it otherwise it will be a waste of your time and effort. The first year we did it, the birds managed to peck holes in it by climbing up and putting their beaks through the wire, making the sheeting like a colander so that when it rained the rain came through and the perches got wet anyway. Roger had to replace it, but first he put hardboard over the top of the wire and the sheeting was placed over this. It was then fastened down round the top edge of the flight.

I always leave a bird bath in the flight during the spring, summer and autumn months in case the birds want to have a proper bath, but it is removed in the wintertime.

REDESIGNING THE AVIARY

I would like to describe here how the aviary was redesigned. Although my birds were compatible during the autumn and winter months after I first acquired them, as soon as the nestboxes were hung up the following spring, I had problems with them which I have described in chapter five. After the breeding season was over, because of the problems, Roger decided to alter things around. He bought another shed the same size as the first, complete with window, and he joined the two sheds together. The new part was insulated in exactly the same way as the original and the whole of the interior painted with white emulsion paint. He partitioned the whole area into separate pens, twelve in all, with removable sides, fronts and bottoms so that in the winter when the nestboxes were removed, the birds could all congregate together if they wanted to and had more room to fly about.

DOUBLE GLAZING

Roger also double-glazed the windows of the shelter for extra protection against the winter elements. He bought two larger panes of glass, fastened them into wooden frames and then screwed them onto the outside shelter walls over the existing windows. This way they can be removed during the warmer months of the year.

BREEDING PENS

In the breeding season, the sides, fronts and bottoms of the pens were replaced, a nestbox and a pair of birds were put in each pen. These pens each measured approximately two feet wide, two and a half feet high and three feet long from front to back. These pens are not all that big but my birds are only confined in them for approximately eight to nine weeks as I only let my birds have one lot of babies per year. We then realised that there was not enough light when the shelter door was closed, so Roger made a glass door which, when it was fastened onto the inside frame, the wooden outer door could also be closed and locked at night. When making a door like this, you should ensure that no draughts can get between the door frame and the door itself. A weather board was also fastened onto the bottom of the glass door to stop any rain from blowing in. By separating the birds in this way, the next breeding season went smoothly without any fights or squabbles.

However, I still was not happy with the situation. I did not like the way the birds were penned up and could not get outside for a fly round even if it was only for a few weeks. I suppose I am too soft hearted but the next year I tried colony breeding again. As the birds had been together for a couple of years now, they seemed even more compatible so I thought it might work this time, especially as they now had more room. I got Roger to put the nestboxes up in the shelter using the whole length of it and not sectioning it off into the individual pens. It did not work. They started squabbling and they all wanted the same nestbox. I do not know why, because all the boxes were identical, perhaps it was the way it was positioned. I left them for about a week but things did not improve and as Jane was ready to lay and still had not sorted out a nestbox, I had to do something quick. After caging them all in separate pens again, Jane laid her first egg of that season within twenty four hours.

SHRUBS AND PLANTS

Since cockatiels will peck shoots off any shrubs or plants as well as gnaw the twigs and bark, it is not practical to grow them in a cockatiel aviary. The birds spoil the appearance of the shrubs and in time the shrubs will die. Apart from which, if the green leaves are eaten, they can cause trouble with the birds' digestion.

MIXING WITH OTHERS

Because cockatiels are all extremely friendly birds, canaries, finches, budgerigars and most dove-like species can be safely housed with them, but personally I would separate all of them in the breeding season just to be on the safe side.

Some budgerigars have a tendency to attack baby cockies and if this should happen, the birds must be separated. Love birds are definitely not recommended as suitable companions as they can be very aggressive towards both adults and babies of other species.

CLEANLINESS

It is best to introduce new birds into the aviary at midday. They will have already eaten in the morning before you acquired them and still have time in the afternoon to find their way about, discover their new food supply and locate a roosting place for the night.

Before any birds were brought into our aviary, I sprayed the whole of the interior of the shelter with Harkers Duramitex, which protects it against red mites for a whole season. You can also mix some of the Duramitex with the emulsion paint.

Cleanliness is an important feature in the aviary. Every day I clean down the shelves or roosting places and once a week wash all the utensils with soap and water, (unless they need doing before). The perches and roosting places are scraped clean and not washed during the winter months otherwise they would not be dry before the birds retired for the night. The loose wood shavings on the floor of the shelter are renewed when necessary. During the summer months, the whole of the interior is washed down, repainted with emulsion (I prefer white, it makes the place look lighter) and re-sprayed with Duramitex. The whole of the outside of the shelter and flight is repainted with Cuprinol or other wood preservative that is harmless to the birds but I leave them shut up in the shelter until the wood is completely dry. An Ioniser is fitted up in the shelter to help remove the dust and other bacteria from the air.

Always keep the doors of both the shelter and flight securely locked at night and when you are away from home, as there are quite a lot of bird thieves around. As an added precaution I have had a burglar alarm installed.

*Dimmer switch control
(courtesy: Sindarins
electronic products)*

CHAPTER 3

BREEDING

COLONY OR SINGLE BREEDING?

Before you start, you have to decide on whether you want to go in for colony or single breeding. Single breeding gives you complete control over each breeding pair and is for the breeder whose aim is serious colour breeding.

The colony system is ideal provided you have established pairs that are not related and the good fortune to own compatible birds. I intended to go in for colony breeding with my birds but as I have already mentioned to you in the last chapter, I had some problems and gave up the idea.

When buying birds for breeding, buy only young specimens if you can, two to three years old is ideal. Beware of low prices because there may be something wrong with the birds. They may be unable to breed, just not want to because they do not like each other, have aggressive natures, be feather pluckers or old birds that are past it.

RULES OF BREEDING

You should not breed related birds and only fully mature birds should be used. The birds should not be allowed to breed until they are at least twelve months old, although if allowed, they will attempt to do so at six months of age. If you have a single bird as a pet, I suggest you keep it as a pet and buy other birds for breeding. Even the most affectionate of pets can sometimes become aggressive when rearing babies. I tried to mate Kim but as I had kept her in the house by herself for two years, with no other birds for company, she did not want to know. She had become too humanised.

When paired off, cockatiels usually stay true to their mates but there is an exception to every rule and this was one of the problems I encountered, described in Chapter 5. Cockatiels can become so attached to each other, the pair bond being so strong, that if one dies the other will scream with grief and spend hours trying to revive its dead mate. When the dead bird is removed there can still be a long period of grieving, so the best thing is to pair him or her off with another bird straight away. I find it quite easy to pair off birds. I just put the chosen pair into a large cage or pen and leave them together for a week or ten days and they usually accept one another. Once you see them preening each other or treading, then you can release them into the aviary where they will usually stay together. Sometimes a pair may not be compatible in which case you will have to try again with other birds.

Get the birds tamed (the author in the colony aviary)

THE BIRD NET AND TAMING

You will need to buy a bird net with which to catch your birds when necessary but catching a bird with a net can be very upsetting for him. Do not thrash the net about wildly, chasing the cockie all over the place but try and act calmly and with experience you should improve.

The best way to tame young birds is to handle them a lot when they are still in the nestbox. Start when they are a couple of weeks old and handle them at least once a day. The parent birds will not mind too much and will not desert them but do not keep the babies out of the box too long, no longer than a few minutes at a time, or they will get chilled.

EYE COLOUR

I would like to point out that if you pair off two white cockatiels, one of them must have brown or black eyes. Do not attempt to mate two whites if they both have red eyes, as their offspring could have eye weaknesses, even blindness.

MATING PROBLEMS

Sometimes you may find that one cock bird wants to do all the mating even though he has his own hen. He will not let any of the other cock birds do any treading at all. If this happens you will have to cage him and his mate for a while keeping them separated the whole breeding season. This of course will only apply if you are trying the colony breeding system.

Some cock birds pluck their hen's feathers from the tops of their heads and from around their necks; some pluck out the red feathers of the hen's cheek patches. It is not harmful to her, it just makes her appear rather unsightly. Sometimes a hen will get even by plucking the cock bird but this only happens occasionally.

A cockatiel in the wild, in its natural environment, usually nests in a hole, a hollow branch or a decaying tree stump but if none of these are available, it will use a live tree. The hen lays her eggs on a large bed of chipped or decaying wood which lies at the bottom of the nesting hole. The nestbox for a cockatiel in an aviary should preferably be made of wood, although cardboard can be used. The advantage of cardboard is that it can be thrown away at the end of the breeding season, the disadvantage being it can be chewed to pieces by the birds in no time at all. I prefer wood for my birds and their first nestboxes measured fifteen inches deep, ten inches wide and ten inches long with a two and a half inch round or square entrance hole near the top. A good firm perch should be fixed just below the entrance hole.

At first, when we tried the colony system, Roger made several nestboxes, all with the same dimensions but with different openings (round and square) near the top so that the birds had a bit of variety, but four pairs out of five seemed to prefer the round hole. In colony breeding, you should always provide more nestboxes than there are breeding pairs of birds, so that the last pair to nest will still have a choice and do not have to settle for what is left. However, this need not apply if you pen the birds separately. I just put a nestbox in the pen and leave the birds to it. A piece of wire netting should be fitted to the inside of the box below the entrance hole (you çan use the same type of wire that was used in constructing the flight) so that the birds can climb in and out more easily. A layer of peat, or wood shavings (not cedar) should be put in the bottom of the box. We use peat and think it is best. Roger also hinged the lids on top of the boxes so we could open them for easy inspection. All nestboxes should be sprayed against red mites before being fastened up in the shelter, I use Harkers Duramitex.

I have a very good friend, Mr Raymond Baxter, who has been a great help to me since I started breeding cockatiels. He has been breeding all kinds of birds for many years and I have picked his brains many times. He made me some smaller nestboxes for my birds' second breeding season, which did not open at the top but had a sliding glass panel at the front covered by another sliding panel made of hardboard. This enabled me to see the birds by sliding the hardboard cover across. To get at the birds, both this cover and the sliding glass panel were removed. Unfortunately, I could not get on with these nestboxes. At the time I had hurt my arm and one day, I slid the panels out to check on the babies and as I was trying to slide the glass panel back into position, I could not get my arm up quickly enough and one of the chicks fell out. Fortunately, it was not hurt but it frightened me so much that the next season I used the nestboxes previously made by Roger.

The birds are usually ready to start breeding in March, (occasionally a pair may start sooner) and the entire breeding cycle takes about two and a half months from the time the eggs are laid until the chicks are weaned. Three to four broods can be produced in one season but I think this is far too many. As my birds are penned up, I only let them have one clutch per season. I like them to get the benefit of the flight and sunshine during the summer months so I take the nestboxes away as soon as the babies are out of them. Any eggs laid afterwards I throw away. The birds go into a moult and by the time the winter is here, their plumage is in fine condition.

Ensure that plenty of grit and cuttlefish are available at all times and when you see the hen constantly at the grit pot and cuttlefish, then you can soon expect eggs.

REARING

When the babies start arriving, give the birds plenty of soft food as well as leafy greens and their normal ration of seed. You can buy dried egg food from pet stores or seed merchants, I use Cede. The parents like a hard boiled egg chopped up occasionally. Do not however feed hard boiled egg too often as it can bind the babies when fed to them by their parents and cause constipation. Please note that the egg must be handled very carefully and kept in a separate dish as stale egg can poison the birds. Any that is leftover should be removed at the end of the day. If you use the colony breeding system, I think it is best to give the hard boiled egg out in the flight, then whatever is leftover at the end of the day or spilt onto the floor, can be cleaned up very easily and thrown away.

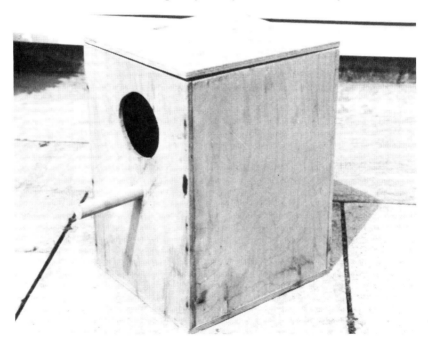

Nest boxes should be capable of easy access

Another recipe is to toast wholewheat bread and crumble it into a dish. Add some millet or baby cereal and a few drops of cod liver oil, mix together and add enough warm water to make it soft and crumbly, not mushy. As an alternative, the wholewheat bread can be moistened with plain water, honey water or glucose and water. This again should be thrown away at the end of the day. Plain cake soaked in milk is also relished by some birds.

Bathing facilities should always be available in the breeding season towards the end of the egg incubation period. The late Robert Stroud (the 'Birdman Of Alcatraz'), mentioned in his book, *Diseases Of Birds*, that he was of the opinion that chicks sometimes die in their shells due to dryness or damp. To eliminate both these possibilities, he suggested that bathing facilities should be withheld during the first ten days of incubation but kept constantly before the hen during the last three days. I let my birds have bathing facilities about a week before the chicks are due to hatch.

One method of preparing egg food

BASIC BREEDING TERMS

The yolk of an egg is the female cell called the ovum and it can be fertilised when it is either in the cavity of the body or just after it enters the oviduct. First of all, one of the eggs separates from the cluster of egg cells that are in the ovary. After six hours, the egg yolk is surrounded by the white or albumen and after another six hours, the shell is formed. Twelve hours later, ovulation takes place and at approximately the same time, a second egg separates from the ovary cluster.

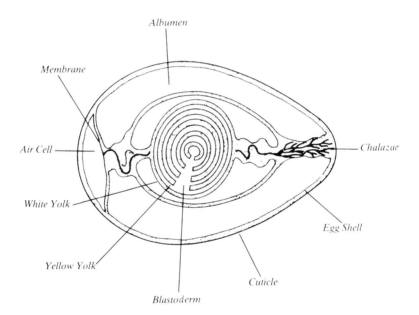

Parts of the egg

EMBRYOLOGY

The egg develops in this way: the first day, the yolk floats in the albumen and by the third day, the tiny heart appears as a tiny red spot. By the sixth day, the extremities and the developing eye can be seen and by the eleventh day, the growing chick starts moving from time to time. Other details such as the toes, are well developed by the thirteenth day and by the sixteenth day the chick is covered in down. By the nineteenth day, it is fully developed and ready to hatch.

The parent birds constantly turn their eggs when sitting on them

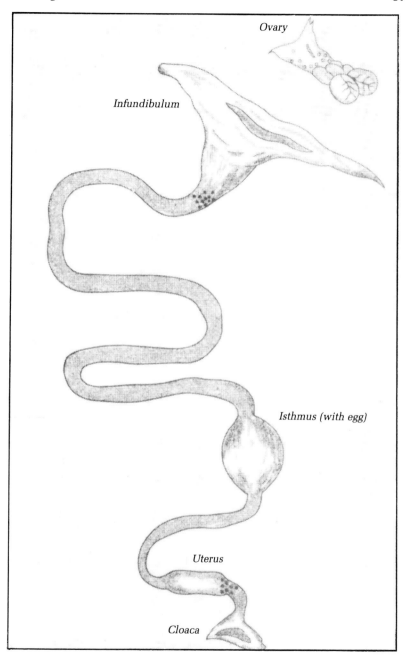

The reproduction system

so that the heat from their bodies is evenly distributed, otherwise the eggs would only develop on one side and the chick would be born deformed. The egg turning stops approximately 48 hours before hatching in response to calls from the baby inside the shell. After hatching, the chick does not need to be fed by its parents for the first twenty four hours as there is enough food in the yolk sac to feed the tiny tot.

It normally takes the chick about 48 hours to break its way out of the shell which can be quite exhausting for the little mite. If it has been pecking regularly for twenty four hours and crying with each peck, it needs help, otherwise it will die. If it is not crying and does not appear to be in any trouble, it should be left alone. If you do have to help, start breaking the shell (with the aid of a toothpick or similar object) where it has already been pecked by the chick, following the circumference of the egg. It is a very slow job and requires a lot of care and plenty of patience so as not to injure the chick inside. Break the shell off in tiny pieces and when the baby is finally free, place it under its mother if she is there, if not, place it in the nestbox and when she hears it crying, hopefully she will return to the box and take over. Sometimes the baby cannot get out because its head is stuck and it can not move it round to peck the shell. If this is the case and you can free its head, place the egg and baby back in the nestbox and it should be able to peck the rest of its way out of the shell.

If you see the hen keep on entering and leaving the nestbox, constantly straining and looking distressed, then she is probably egg bound. You can do several things to try and help her. Try putting her in a box covered with a wire grid, in a temperature of 85 degrees F, after first putting a few drops of warmed olive oil in her vent. Also put a few drops of the oil in her beak. An infra-red lamp can be used and you can supply extra warmth by placing a heating pad under the box, the sort used in wine making is ideal. A few drops of glycerine in her drinking water may also help. You can try a hot water bottle covered with a cloth and sit her on this or try steaming her. To steam her, put some hot water in a deep pan, tie a cloth over the top and sit the hen on it. What you are trying to do is to get her to relax and she should pass the egg in between twenty and sixty minutes, but whatever method you try, be very careful that you do not burn the bird. If after an hour no egg has been delivered, seek the advice of a veterinary surgeon, as drugs can be used but the hen must have medical attention within twelve hours. When treating the bird yourself, be very careful that the egg does not break inside her as the sharp shell can cause fatal injuries.

PAIRING UP

When birds are first introduced to each other, it can take a few weeks before the pair get started. The eggs usually appear in the nestbox fifteen to twenty days after mating takes place, the hen laying every other day. The number of eggs per clutch can range between three and ten, the larger clutches being laid by the older, more mature hens although on occasions, a first year hen will lay an enormous clutch but these rarely hatch out. I had a white hen who in her first season laid twenty eggs and although both she and her mate took turns at sitting on them for the whole twenty one days, not one of the eggs hatched out. When I broke the eggs open, most of them were what is known as dead in shell.

EGGS

Cockatiel eggs are white, glossy and oval in shape. The incubation period for each egg is approximately twenty to twenty one days but the eggs do not start developing until they reach the same temperature as the body temperature of the parent birds which can take up to

Eggs are white, glossy and oval in shape

three days. The cock bird usually sits during the day from dawn to the late afternoon and the hen from late afternoon to the following dawn. The two of them usually spend some time together out of the nest box during the late afternoon until the hen goes in for the night. Sometimes, the birds are so devoted they both sit together in the nestbox. If you find any eggs not being incubated, try to place them under other breeding birds. Sometimes the birds will not start sitting straight away but this is no cause for alarm provided they commence sitting within ten days. If after ten days, the birds show no sign of sitting, then you can either throw them away and hope that the next clutch will be incubated or you can place them with other birds that have eggs of their own. If no other birds are available and you do not want to throw the eggs away, then you will have to consider hand rearing.

If any eggs are found to be stuck together or to the bottom of the nestbox with dirt or droppings, then they should be gently freed. You can use a cloth soaked in warm water but the eggs must be thoroughly dried afterwards to prevent chilling. if the eggs are not stuck, do not clean them just because they are dirty. They will not hurt being dirty and you may do more harm than good.

WATCHING THE EGGS

To test the eggs for fertility, hold them up either to the sunlight or an electric light bulb. There should be a small dark speck at first and red veins that run in all directions. As the chick develops the egg fills up and becomes darker in colour. If the chick dies in the shell, part of the egg will be clear and there will be a dark lump. If after six days the egg still looks clear, it may be infertile and therefore no good. However, do not throw any eggs away too soon. The parent birds usually stop sitting as soon as they know that the eggs are no good or that the chicks have died. It amazes me how they know but most of them do. Once you remove the eggs the hen should start laying again. You can do a test to see if the chick is alive. Put the egg in a cup of warm water and if it is alive the chick will kick but do not leave the egg in the water for more than a couple of minutes or the baby will drown.

FEEDING THE YOUNG

When the eggs begin hatching, you will hear a squeaking noise from the babies in the nestbox. When newly hatched they look ugly little things, covered with long yellowish silky down. The parents do not mind the nestbox being inspected provided it is not done too often. It is very rare for cockatiels to desert their young due to the nestboxes being interfered with. They take equal care of all their chicks and if good parents, even the smallest rarely comes to any harm.

I have found that when feeding their chicks, my birds consume large quantities of sunflower seeds which are regurgitated and fed to their youngsters. They also drink an enormous amount of water. Therefore, it is advisable to keep a constant supply of both these items before the parent birds at all times. As the babies develop, the parents feed more canary seed and millet and less of the egg food. Soaked seed is also appreciated.

Well fed chicks look overfed to the inexperienced person. If the crop is stuffed with hard seed and is not big and soft, if the baby has a dried up look, its pin feathers look flat and the eyes are not open by the seventh or eighth day, then you are in for trouble. The babies are not developing as quickly as they should be and not getting enough nutrition from their parent's regurgitated seed. If hard seed is seen in the chicks' crop, offer more leafy greens and plenty of soft food to the parent birds. If they will not eat it, just provide them with sunflower seeds, soft food and greens and take away all other hard seed.

About a fortnight after the babies have hatched, the nestbox will have become very soiled and needs to be cleaned out. When the parents are out of the box, remove the chicks and place them in a small dish or container lined with a towel or similar article, (whatever it is, it must be closely woven material so that the chicks do not catch their claws in it). Quickly scrape out the box and put in clean dry peat, shavings or whatever it is you are using. Check that there are no droppings or food stuck to the chicks' feet, legs or beak. Because the babies grow so quickly, if droppings are allowed to dry on their extremities, they can grow deformed and this is one of the reasons that the chicks should be checked each day after the parents have ceased to brood them. If the babies are badly soiled remove the dirt with cotton wool soaked in warm water. Do not drop the chicks and above all do not soak them. Get them back into the nestbox as quickly as possible.

As previously stated, the chicks grow very quickly, their pin feathers appearing when they are about a week old. These feathers appear first on the wings, tail and crest and then on the abdomen, back and crop. The chicks are fully feathered and ready to leave the nestbox when they are about four and a half weeks to five weeks old, but the parents continue to feed them for a further ten to fourteen days after leaving the nestbox. You should not remove them from the parent birds until you are sure they can fend for themselves.

Dishes for soaking seed

FEATHER PLUCKING

Sometimes the parents abuse their chicks by feather plucking them.
If this happens, you should separate the chicks from their parents as
soon as they appear to be picking up and eating food themselves.
You can do one of two things: when the chicks eventually come out
of the nestbox, give them millet sprays to eat as this is the easiest
seed for them to learn to shell. After a few days when you see them
eating the millet without much trouble, take the chicks away from
their parents. Take them away in the morning after the parents have
fed them, put them in a separate pen in full view of their parents,
leave them there all day with plenty of millet sprays, grit and water
in addition to other seeds and greens, until the late afternoon. You
can then return them to their parents so that they can feed them
again before they settle down for the night. Do this each day for
about a week, then separate them completely from their parents until
all of their feathers have regrown. They can then be released into the
flight with the other birds. If you do not want to go to all this trouble,

A problem can be dead in shell chicks. Many possible reasons apply: 1. Inadequate diet 2. Weak parents 3. Lack of moisture 4. Uncertain climatic conditions 5. Hen being disturbed

you can leave them with their parents for about three weeks after they have left the nestbox (by which time they should be feeding themselves without any trouble but watch out for late starters), then separate them from their parents until all of their feathers have regrown. Once they are fully feathered up (usually this takes about four weeks) and allowed to mix with the other birds it is most unlikely that their parents will pluck them as badly again. Occasionally, when the youngsters are returned to the flight and meet up with their parents once more, you can get the odd bird that plucks a few feathers off the top of its babies head, but it doesn't happen very often.

HAND REARING

Sometimes a chick has to be fostered or hand-reared. If a parent stops feeding a chick, then it has to be taken away from them. If it is possible, place the baby in a nest with other chicks of the same age otherwise the foster parents may refuse to feed a much younger chick and it will be left to die.

If you find a chick that looks dead, it may still be alive even if it is cold and shows no sign of life. Try breathing on him and warming him in your hands. If you manage to revive it put it back in the nestbox and the parents should soon take care of him again. I put my apparently dead chicks in a dish which is lined and loosely covered with a cloth, on the plate warming rack of the gas cooker. I light the gas and leave it turned on *very low*. If the chick is alive, the warmth will revive him in a couple of minutes and he will start squeaking.

Hand rearing in my opinion is not easy if the chick is less than one week old. After a week you stand a better chance of rearing one but it is time consuming and you need a lot of patience. It is very rewarding if you manage to save just one chick but you must be prepared for some if not all of your babies to die. I managed to rear one until his pin feathers started to grow and then I lost him, I found him dead one morning when I returned from shopping. The following year I had another go, this time hand rearing one from the age of eight days and I was successful. I will tell you more about this later.

First of all set up an incubator, which should be kept at a constant temperature of 95 degrees. You can make one yourself from a wooden box with a fifteen watt bulb inside but the bulb must be covered so that the chick does not come into contact with it. Here again you could use an infra-red lamp, or you could try my method described later on in this chapter. Handle the baby as little as possible or he will get chilled. When picking up a baby bird, you should never pick it up without supporting its legs. If the chick's legs dangle down it will make him feel very insecure. You should lift him with one hand and slip the upturned palm of your other hand underneath him so that his feet are secure in your hand. Feed him little and often and wrap him in a towel when you fetch him out of the incubator to feed him, to keep him warm.

Use a 10cc syringe without the needle for a cockatiel, the opening cut off to enable the mixture to get through. Put the mixture into the large end of the syringe and push through slowly, just into his beak *over* his tongue, being careful not to let any air bubbles form. Hold the chick's head between your thumb and index finger as you feed it. You may find you do better with an eye-dropper instead of a syringe, I know I did, or you can feed with a small spoon, but the food must be runny enough to slide off the spoon easily.

Before giving food to the chick, you should test the temperature of the food with your lips or the inside of your wrist just like you would do for a human baby. If it is too hot it will burn the youngster and if it is too cold he will not like it and will refuse to eat it. One way is to put the mixture into a small wine glass and put the glass inside a cup of very hot water. When the water has cooled the food should be ready. You could also use an egg poacher in which to keep the food warm.

Don't keep on feeding the chick until he stops squeaking as he doesn't know when he has had enough and you may overfeed him. A lot of baby chicks die from being overfed. Feed him until he has a full crop but be very careful that the food does not go down into his windpipe. Try and keep the air out but if air does get into the crop, burp the chick. To do this, slowly massage the crop from the bottom upwards. Don't rub but work the air bubble up through the throat until it burps.

Clean any food off the youngster's beak as dried-on food can cause the beak to grow deformed. Wait until the crop is empty before giving him the next feed. Any unused food should be refrigerated. It will thicken when it becomes cold but it can be thinned down by adding a little warm water. Yogurt should be added to any food given as it is a good source of bacteria which is needed by the chick to help break down the food in the digestive tract. The food is then more easily absorbed.

As the chick grows older you should change from a syringe or eye-dropper to a plastic teaspoon if you are not already using one. Warm a plastic quarter teaspoon over an open flame and with a pair of pliers squeeze the top of the spoon into a V shape.

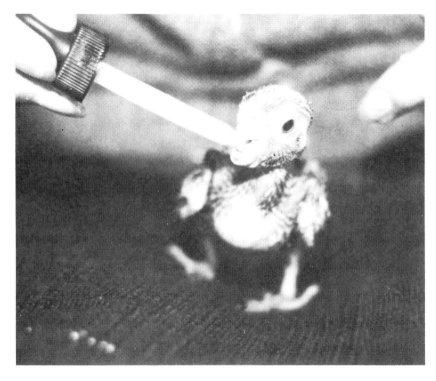

Charlie at two and a half weeks being fed by a dropper

WEANING

You should begin weaning at seven to eight weeks. Feed the baby by hand in the morning and leave seed, millet, water, grit and some of the formula handy so that he can help himself during the day. Hand feed him again at night before he goes to bed. At ten weeks of age you should only need to feed him once a day.

A PERSONAL EXPERIENCE

I will now tell you about the baby bird that I managed to hand rear. Roger called it Charlie but it turned out to be a hen. One evening about five o'clock I found the youngest of Jane's four babies, which was about eight days old, lying on the bottom of the nestbox, still alive but very weak. There was no food in its crop so I brought it into the house and fed it by way of an eye-dropper, little and often for about three hours. I gave it a mixture of Weetabix made with water, honey and peanut butter, mixed to a puree. The baby took to the dropper and after three hours, it was sitting up and appeared quite

Cockatiels mature quickly so a sound diet is essential. Charlie at 8 weeks of age

strong again. I decided to put it back in the nestbox with the other chicks hoping that Jane would now take over and carry on looking after it. The next morning it was lying down again, weak and unfed. I brought it back into the house and decided to try and hand rear the little mite although I had no incubator.

First of all while she was so weak, I put the chick in a dish which I lined with a warm piece of material. I covered the material with a piece of newspaper and covered the dish over with a towel leaving a small opening to give the chick air and for her to see out if she wanted to. The dish was placed on top of a heating tray, the kind used in wine making. This way the dish kept warm without getting too hot and burning the baby.

For the first few days, I fed her on the following formula:

2 tablespoons Weetabix made with water
2 tablespoons sunflower seeds (shelled – obtainable from
   health shops)

2 tablespoons brown bread crumbs
1 hard boiled egg
1 tablespoon plain yogurt
1 tablespoon honey
Small scraping cuttlefish
Few drops of Abidec.

The whole lot was mixed together, made into a puree of a runny consistency and fed to the chick with an eye-dropper. I fed her every three to four hours, the last feed at night at around eleven o'clock and the first one in the morning at around five thirty. I did not feed her during the night. When she wanted feeding during the day she usually told me in her way and there was no way I could overfeed her, as when she had had enough she clamped her beak tight shut and turned her head away.

I found that first thing in the morning she had to be coaxed to eat but as the day wore on her appetite improved. After a few days when her system had become accustomed to her new diet, the chick became too strong to keep her in the dish, so I brought in a clean nestbox, lined it in the same way as I had lined the dish and placed the nestbox on the piece of wood that rested on the heating tray. I also gave the baby a change in menu. I still gave my formula but for alternate meals, I gave her Milupa Infant Food obtainable from chemists. The varieties she had were Winter Casserole and Autumn Fruits.

The baby went from strength to strength. I started weaning her at seven weeks of age by giving her chopped, hard boiled egg, shelled sunflower seeds, chickweed and soaked, clipped oats, gradually reducing the number of feeds I was giving her. She went on to millet sprays and canary seed, both soaked for twenty four hours previously. At nine weeks I was just feeding her first thing in the morning and last thing at night, during the day she fed herself. At ten weeks she was completely weaned.

DESERTION

If your parent birds desert their eggs, you will have to decide whether to lose the eggs, place them under other hens if possible or try and hatch them yourself in an incubator and hand rear the chicks. In my opinion, placing them under other breeding hens if you have any, is the best course of action. If you do decide to have a go yourself there are several types of incubators on the market to choose from. Some of them are rather expensive but there are cheaper models available. The temperature in the incubator is gradu-ally brought up to 101 degrees F. by the end of the first day and 102 degrees F. by the end of the second day and leave it at this until the eggs have hatched. If your incubator does not have an automatic spraying and turning device, then you will have to spray the eggs daily with luke warm water and turn them twice every twenty four hours. When hatched, the chicks should be put in a small box which should be heated as previously described in this chapter.

RINGING BIRDS

If you wish to ring your baby birds, you should do so on the seventh or eighth day. It is best to ring them in the evening before the hen covers the chicks for the night. Metal rings are best as cockatiels can chew up plastic ones. The chick should be held in one hand with one leg held between the thumb and first finger. The two front toes are brought together, the ring is slipped over these two toes and then over the two back toes which are held back against the leg. You can rub Vaseline onto the chick's legs and feet so that the ring slides on more easily but once the ring is in place, you must wipe the Vaseline off so nothing else sticks to the chick after you have returned it to the nestbox. If you only want to ring the chicks for your own identifica-tion purposes, then you can use the removable plastic ones. Watch that the hen does not throw both the ring and the chick out of the nestbox. She does not realise that the ring is attached to her baby. All she knows is that there is a foreign object in her nest so out it must go. If the chick is thrown out and is found on the floor of the pen, stiff and cold, try and revive it by warming it up. You could try my gas cooker method. Once revived the chick can be returned to the nestbox and in a few hours, will be as good as new. Personally, I do not like the idea of ringing birds so I do not ring mine.

FAILURE TO BREED

If after two or three months your birds have not started breeding, it may be due to one of several reasons. They may not be one hundred per cent fit. They may have colds, mites, sore feet, be immature or just do not like each other. If mating takes place and no eggs have been laid in three to four months, it is possible that there is some-thing wrong with the hen and she cannot lay. If eggs are laid and are always clear, then it is possible that the cock bird is sterile but this is not always the case. Sometimes it is a simple thing that can often be put right. For example, the perches may not be fixed firmly enough or they may be set too high and the cock bird keeps banging his head on the roof of the pen. You will have to determine the cause and correct it. If after three years you are still not having any success, I would suggest that you try changing one of your birds or even both of them.

CHAPTER 4

COLOURS AND MUTATIONS

I would like to describe the different colours and mutations that I have in my aviary. Apart from normal greys, I have whites, pieds, pearls, pearl-pied, cinnamon-pearl-pied and cinnamons, quite a few of them split for other colours. As I have already described the grey in Chapter 1, I will move on to the white or albino.

See colour section for examples of the main colours.

WHITE OR ALBINO

The cock bird should be pure white except for the front of his head, throat and cheeks which are yellow and his crest feathers can be a mixture of yellow and white or as in some mutations, all yellow. He has orange-red ear patches on his cheeks, like the grey, but there are yellow areas on his tail and wings. The eyes are red in pure albinos but they can be red, brown, black or grey in other white mutations, although a black-eyed white is not very common. The beak is a biscuit colour and the feet and legs are pale pink. An albino is a totally white bird with red or pink eyes and pink feet, lacking any other colour.

The white hen has the same colouring as the cock bird, but she has yellow on her thighs and under her tail. Her ear patches are also orange-red but are supposed to be less bright in colour than those of the cock bird. However, some of the white hens that I have bred have had ear patches brighter than most cock birds.

The youngsters do not have as much yellow on them as the adults and their eyes appear to be a lighter shade of red and much brighter.

They are difficult to sex until they are fully mature. A fully matured hen can be told by the polka dots on the underside of her flight feathers, the cock bird losing his when he reaches maturity. Sometimes, the sex of a white hen is known straight away because genetically the parent birds can only produce white hens, for example a pearl hen paired to an albino cock bird produce white hens and grey cock birds, the cock birds being split for both albino and pearl. A white hen inherits her colouring from her father regardless of the colour of her mother, but a white male must have a white mother, as well as a white or split-white father.

LUTINOS

There are also white birds that are not pure white in colour, but have extra yellow colouring on their bodies and wings, although their colouring is the same as the albino in every other way. These birds are called lutinos. Some of them are often a strong primrose yellow with a primrose body and a daffodil yellow face.

PIED

The pied cock bird is very similar to the normal grey but he has different markings of white and yellow, which break up the grey colouring. He has the same orange-red cheek patches and a yellow crest. His beak is grey, his eyes are brown and his tail can be all yellow or a mixture of yellow and black feathers. The outer flight feathers on his wings can be either yellow or grey and the feet can be either grey or pink. I've known one pied to have different coloured feet, one foot grey and the other pink. My pied Matthew has different coloured claws on his feet, half of them are black and the other half pink.

The pied hen is very similar in colouring to the cock bird although her orange-red cheek patches are not usually as bright in colour. The underside of her tail is usually striped yellow and black, the same as a normal grey-hen. The youngsters are like the hen, only paler in colouring but their colour deepens as they grow older.

The markings on the pieds vary from bird to bird, you never seem to get two exactly the same. My Heidi has a very black face.

PEARL

A pearl cockatiel is similar in body colouring to that of a normal grey but there are large areas on the wings which are speckled with white and yellow. They also have orange-red cheek patches, which are not so bright in colour as those of a grey and their crests do not appear to be such a bright yellow. The eyes are brown, the beak is grey and the feet and legs can be grey or pink. The hen has no white at the sides of her crown and the underside of her tail is striped with yellow and grey.

The male birds gradually lose the speckled effect on their wings each time they moult and eventually revert to normal grey colouring. The hen bird keeps her speckled appearance for life.

CINNAMON

The cinnamon cock bird is a fawny shade, the darker colouring being on the underside of his tail. His face, throat and cheeks are yellow and his crest is a mixture of yellow and grey/brown feathers. He has white at the sides of his crown like the normal grey and there is a band of white, tinted with some pale yellow, on the edge of his folded wings. His cheek patches are also orange-red, his eyes are brown, his beak is dark grey and his feet and legs are pink.

The hen has similar colouring to that of the cock bird but her cheek patches are not so bright. There is no white at the sides of her crown and the yellow on her face and throat is usually only faintly tinted. My Amy, however, has such a bright yellow face people often mistake her for a cock bird. The cinnamon hen has yellow on her thighs and the underside of her tail is striped with grey/brown and yellow. Their colouring seems to deepen as they grow older.

The youngsters are like the hen, only paler in colour and, like the normal grey, do not begin to show yellow on their faces until they are several months old. Last year I noticed that one of the nestlings had red eyes for the first few weeks, then they turned brown. Until it feathered up I thought it was going to be an albino. I do not know if this is a common occurrence but I have never noticed it before.

COLOUR BREEDING

Regarding colour breeding, I can only give you some examples of what colours can be bred from pairing my birds together.

The process is learned gradually when it comes to the X and Y chromosomes. I give a simple explanation about **recessive** and **dominant** factors but this book is mainly aimed at giving general information on the care and welfare of the birds.

A male bird, normal in colour can carry an invisible colour factor, this factor being called **recessive**. These birds are called splits, the invisible colour being hidden inside their genes. A visible colour factor is known as the **dominant** factor.

It is understandable that a white mated to another white will produce white offspring and normal grey to normal grey results in grey babies. Mate pied to pied and the results should be one hundred per cent pied. However, if a normal grey cock bird is mated to a white hen, all their babies should be grey in colour. There should be equal numbers of cock birds and hens over several nests, (grey being the dominant factor), the cock birds being split for white, (recessive factor) and the hens being pure greys. Timothy and Zoe produce these offspring.

Matthew, a pied cock bird paired to Jane, a normal grey hen, produce all grey young but their babies, both cock birds and hens, are split for pied.

Adam, who is a pied cock bird split for albino and Katy, his albino hen produce grey cock birds and hens, albino cock birds and hens and all the youngsters are split for pied.

Benjamin, a pied cock bird split for pearl and albino has Amy, a cinnamon hen for his mate and they produce grey cock birds and hens, albino and pearl hens with some of the cock birds being split for albino, pearl and cinnamon.

Danny, an albino cock bird mated to Emma, a pearl hen, produced on an average four to five albino hens and two grey cock birds, split for albino in each clutch. Last year they excelled themselves. They had six albino hens and two grey cock birds in one clutch and reared all eight. They also fostered two pied chicks at the same time and these also lived. The nestbox, having ten growing chicks in it was so full the parents could not get in the box with them, they had to stand in the opening and bend down inside the box to feed them all.

When Danny died, I obtained another white cock bird as a mate for Emma and also called this one Danny. Now this cock bird must be split for pearl as they have produced not only grey cock birds and albino hens, but pearl of both sexes.

James, a normal grey cock bird split for pied, has Wendy a white hen for his mate. For the last four years, they have always produced grey youngsters, cock birds and hens. The cock birds are split for albino and the hens for pied. However, this year for the very first time, they have produced three pieds, one hen and two cock birds so Wendy the white mother must also be split for pied.

Another pied cock bird, Joseph, has a normal grey hen, Becky, for his mate. As Becky is split for pied, their youngsters are grey cock birds and hens and pied cock birds and hens in equal numbers, the greys being split for pied.

Nicolas, another pied cock bird is paired to Susan, a pearl pied hen. Their youngsters are all pied, the cock birds being split for pearl.

A normal grey cock bird, if split for cinnamon and paired to a cinnamon hen, should produce 50 per cent cinnamon cock birds and hens and 50 per cent normal grey cock birds and hens, the cock birds being split for cinnamon.

Scott, a cinnamon cock bird who has Lisa, a pearl hen for his mate, produce 50 per cent grey cook birds split for cinnamon and pearl and 50 per cent cinnamon hens. A white cock bird paired to a cinnamon hen will produce albino hens and grey cock birds, the cock birds being split for cinnamon and albino.

Peter, a white cock bird split for pied has Heidi, a pied hen for his mate. They have not yet had any youngsters but they should produce grey cock birds and white hens, pied cock birds and hens. Both the grey and pied cock birds being split for albino.

PROBLEMS WITH SPLITS

These days with all the splits around you never know what youngsters to expect in a nestbox, unless you keep a strict control over colour. For example, Guy, a grey cock bird split for albino and pearl and Mandy, his grey hen split for pied, never have two clutches the same. The first year their clutch consisted of all grey babies, two hens and two cock birds. The second year they had one grey cock bird, one albino hen and two pearl hens. In the third year clutch they produced two grey cock birds and two albino hens. Some of the hens would be split for pied and some of the cock birds would be split for pied, pearl or albino.

Another example, Simon a grey cock bird split for cinnamon, pied and pearl and Rachel, a cinnamon pearl hen split for pied, will produce mixed results over a number of nests. The baby cock birds could be normal greys split for cinnamon pearl, normal greys split for cinnamon pearl and pied, cinnamons split for pearl, pearl pieds split for cinnamon and pearls split for cinnamon, some of which will be split for pied. The young hens could be cinnamon pied, pearl pied and cinnamon pearl of which some will be split for pied.

A hen can be split for pied, but not for albino, pearl or cinnamon, as these last three are all sex-linked and sex-linked hens cannot be split.

A pearl pied can be either primrose yellow or white, except the grey on the wings is replaced by pearl markings.

A cinnamon pearl has yellow markings on cinnamon or fawn colour plumage and the crest and tail are cinnamon and yellow.

A cinnamon pied is similar in colouring to the pied but the grey is replaced by a lovely cinnamon or fawn shade.

A cinnamon pied pearl can be either white or yellow. The crest is yellow and the tail is also yellow but barred with grey-fawn underneath. The wings are white or yellow and the back and breast clear. Cock birds revert to the cinnamon and yellow or white of a pied cockatiel once they start to moult.

A normal grey cock bird split for pearl and albino paired to a cinnamon pied hen will produce grey cock birds split for pearl, cinnamon and pied. Grey cock birds split for albino, cinnamon and pied. Pearl hens and albino hens, both split for pied.

A normal grey cock bird split for albino and pearl paired to a white hen will produce grey cock birds split for pearl and albino and albino cock birds. The hens will be pearl and and albino.

A pied cock bird split for cinnamon and pearl paired to a cinnamon split for pied hen will produce young cock birds, cinnamon pied, cinnamon split for pied, normal grey split for pearl, cinnamon and pied, and pied split for pearl and cinnamon. The hens will be cinnamon pied, cinnamon split for pied, pearl pied and pearl split for pied.

A normal grey cock bird split for pearl and albino paired to a cinnamon split for pied hen will produce cock birds, normal grey split for pearl and cinnamon, pied split for pearl and cinnamon, normal grey split for albino and cinnamon and pied split for albino and cinnamon. The hens will be pearl, pearl pied and albino pied.

A normal grey cock bird split for pearl and albino paired to a albino hen will produce cock birds, normal grey split for pearl and albino, normal grey split for albino, pearl and pied, albino and albino split for Pied. The young hens will be pearl, pearl split for pied, albino and albino split for pied.

LUTINO PEARLS

These are very beautiful birds with yellow pearling on the white or primrose yellow feathers. The cock bird reverts to pure lutino after a few months but hens, as with all pearls, keep their lovely markings for life.

SILVER OR DILUTE

The main body colouring of these birds is various shades of bright silver-grey with the deeper tones being on the undersides of the tail. The front of the head, cheeks and throat are lemon-yellow and the crest is a mixture of yellow and silver-grey feathers.

NEW MUTATIONS

New mutations continue to appear on the scene; one of the latest is the white-faced which does not display the normal orange cheek patches. The most recent is the pastel-faced. Instead of a yellow face with orange patches, they have a pale lemon face with a very pale cheek patch. It is so recent that at the time of writing its genetic make-up is not known.

CHAPTER 5

DAY TO DAY PROBLEMS

In an earlier chapter I mentioned that I had encountered a few problems when I began to breed cockatiels. I will now describe these problems in more detail and explain how I overcame them, in case any of my readers encounter the same.

INTRODUCING PAIRS

The first pair that I owned were Daniel, a white cock bird and Emma, his pearl or opaline hen. They had the aviary to themselves for the first three weeks which was a mistake. Then I introduced the next pair, Simon and Amy, both cinnamons. Danny would not let them have any food or use any of the nest boxes. He thought the whole aviary belonged to Emma and himself and that the other two birds were intruders. I had to take both pairs out of the aviary and put them in cages for a few days while Roger, (my husband, you remember) altered the interior of the shelter (moving perches, taking down the nestboxes etc) so that when the birds were re-introduced to it, it would appear different to them. I bought another pair of birds, Adam, a split pied and Katy, his white hen and put all three pairs of birds into the aviary at the same time and they settled down happily together.

Some weeks later I bought a normal grey pair, Timothy and Jane, off my friend Ray but when I put them into my aviary, Timothy did not want to know Jane. He fancied Katy the white hen so I decided to buy another white hen and see if he would take to her. This I did and named her Heidi. I caged her up with Timothy for a few days, they

Left: Normal Grey hen
Below: Pearl-pied hen

Left: White cock
Below: White hen
Note the distinctive
orange spot

accepted one another and I then returned them to the aviary. I now had to find a new mate for Jane and eventually found Matthew, a pied. I caged him and Jane the same as I did Timothy and Heidi and they also accepted one another and were returned to the aviary.

BREEDING DIFFICULTIES

I have already mentioned in chapter two that my birds were very compatible all through the autumn and winter months sharing the same shelter and flight, but further problems arose when Roger put up the nestboxes the following spring for them to colony-breed.

Matthew would not let any of the other male birds tread their hens. Each time they attempted to do this, he flew at them and knocked them off. He did not want to tread the other hens himself, he had Jane and was quite happy with her, in fact he was devoted to her. I've never found out just why he does this and did not know how to stop him.

I thought that if Jane went down with with eggs first, Matthew would take his turn at sitting on them and this would give the other pairs a chance to mate. However, one afternoon after arriving home from work, I noticed that there was something wrong with Matthew. He looked as if he had suffered a stroke. The left side of his face looked as if it had been flattened, even his eye looked flat instead of rounded and his left wing hung down low at his side although it was not broken. I brought him and Jane into the house where it was warm, caged and kept them where I could keep an eye on Matthew for a few days.

After about a week I noticed an improvement and another week later his face and wing were better and the left eye was rounded again. I decided to return him and Jane to the aviary the next morning, but that night Jane laid an egg on the floor of the cage. Roger fitted a nestbox onto the side of the cage, I put the egg inside the box and Jane went straight in and over the next few days she laid three more eggs. The eggs eventually hatched but two of the chicks died, each one at the age of ten days.

I took the bodies to the vet for a post mortem and he thought it was a yolk sac infection and prescribed Terramycin in the drinking water. He also suggested that I scrub out and disinfect the nestbox. As I had an identical nestbox that had never been used, I decided to swap the boxes over, thinking that a scrubbed out one would be damp. Roger swapped them over for me and I put the two remaining chicks inside. No way would Jane go in that box, not even at night. Matthew went in but soon came out again..As cock birds do not sit at night and Jane had no intention of doing so, I was worried to death about the chicks, thinking they might get chilled. I phoned my friend Ray who came round straight away. He had a look at the chicks and said they had sufficient food in their crops to last them through the night and with them being in the house they would be warm enough, but he advised me to put the original nestbox back after I had cleaned it out. Apparently Jane knew it was not her box although it was identical in size and shape to the one she had been using. I did what he advised and after I had put the original nestbox back the next day, Jane went in to her chicks. The Terramycin was put in the drinking water and the remaining two chicks survived. They were both hens and one of them became so tame I decided to keep her and called her Mandy.

MONOPOLISING THE SHELTER

The next problem involved Timothy again. He wanted the whole shelter for himself and Heidi and would not let any of the other birds back inside the shelter after they had gone out into the flight. Timothy remained inside the shelter all day with Heidi and when any of the other birds entered the bobhole from outside, he attacked them. I could not let him get away with this so I brought him and Heidi into the house, caged them and put them in the same room with Matthew and Jane.

Heidi looked fat with eggs so Roger fitted a nestbox to their cage. However, poor Heidi did not survive her first breeding season. The first egg she laid seemed perfectly normal but she then laid another one which had no shell. It was just like a piece of soft rubber and I found it on the floor of the cage and not in the nestbox.

The next two eggs again seemed perfectly normal. On the day she died I was at work. Roger was at home that day and he phoned me at the office later that morning to see if I could go home. Heidi was not well and he did not know what to do to help her. He thought she was egg bound and had tried steaming her but it did not help. I went straight home but she died before I got there. The vet said she had died trying to lay another 'rubber' egg and there was nothing I could have done. He was surprised that she had managed to lay the first 'rubber' one.

I then had to get Timothy another mate so I bought another white hen the next day, named her Zoe, caged her with Timothy for a few days and they accepted one another without any problems. I tried putting Heidi's normal eggs under another hen but they did not hatch.

Above: White-faced Cockatiels
Below: Kim, a normal Cockatiel, eating crumbs

Wendy, a lutino with primrose colouring

SELFISH BIRDS

Sometimes you will find that a cock bird wants more than one hen. This is the trouble I experienced with Adam. His hen Katy went down with eggs but instead of taking his turn at sitting on them during the day, he went after Amy, the cinnamon hen who was Simon's mate. Adam started treading Amy, (the little madam was quite willing) and although Simon tried to intervene, Adam was too bossy for him. Eventually, Amy laid her eggs and Adam started sitting on them. Simon wanted to sit on them himself (after all Amy was his mate and he thought the eggs belonged to him) but Adam attacked him and would not let him go in the nestbox. They kept fighting and little Simon came off worse every time. I did not have any more spare cages so Roger partitioned off part of the shelter. I shut Adam and Katy in the one part together with their nestbox and eggs and after a couple of days, Adam took his turn at sitting.

Simon was now a lot happier because he could help Amy incubate her eggs without any interference, but now that he had got his confidence back, he started to attack Danny and Emma. There was no way Roger could partition the shelter off again so he put a board up between their nestboxes so that they could not see one another. This seemed to do the trick and peace reigned at last. They all got down to the serious business of raising their babies.

CASE STUDIES

The next season the aviary was altered and the birds penned up but I still had some problems. The first involved Katy. Over a period of several weeks she laid twenty eggs (three clutches) and not one of the eggs hatched. The chicks all died in their shells on the point of hatching. I never did find out the reason why. I thought when the first clutch failed to hatch that the eggs were too dry so I sprayed the second clutch with water every day for the last ten days of incubation. It made no difference and they too failed to hatch. The third clutch also failed but thinking about it later, I remembered that Katy had eaten a lot of sunflower seeds prior to laying her eggs and I suppose it is possible that the chicks were too fat and therefore could not turn round in the shells to peck their way out. I shall never know but since then I have always made sure that my birds do not have a lot of sunflower seeds just prior to the breeding season. As I have had very few dead in shell since then off any of my birds (and I now have twelve breeding pairs), there may be something in it. However, going back to my tale, the following season Katy's eggs hatched normally and her babies were perfectly healthy.

I kept one of my baby hens that year, a pearl I named Lisa. I had intended to keep her as a spare hen but she kept laying infertile eggs on the floor of the shelter and sitting on them. All the other birds had mates and she wanted one.

About the same time that this was happening, I lost Simon the cinnamon with Hepatitis. He had been perfectly well on the Saturday, in fact he had been treading Amy that same morning. On Sunday he did not seem very well so I brought the pair of them into the house where it was warmer and I could also keep an eye on him. I would like to mention here that if ever you have a sick bird and you separate it from the other birds, always put its mate with it. If you do not want to keep it in the same cage, place it in another cage alongside that of its sick mate as sometimes they pine for each other and this can prolong the illness.

Now, getting back to Simon, I thought he might have a chill and as I did not have a hospital cage, I increased the temperature of the room where he was to 90 degrees F. but the warmth did not help in this case. During the Sunday afternoon he grew progressively worse. He just sat on the edge of his water pot with his eyes closed, breathing heavily, his droppings just like pools of water. As I had not any antibiotics to give him I decided to take him to the vet the following morning. However, when morning came I found him dead on the floor of the cage. I took his body to the vet for a post mortem and it was found he had died of jaundice caused by the Hepatitis.

I bought another cinnamon cock bird split for pied as a mate for Amy straight away so she would not grieve too much and I named him Scott. Amy however had other ideas and would not have anything to do with him, so I put him with Lisa, the pearl hen and they paired off. Unfortunately, their first lot of chicks only lived for a few days. I did not realise at the time but they were not feeding them properly. By the time I did find out it was too late. I think Lisa was too young and inexperienced and Scott could not manage by himself. He seemed to be feeding the chicks but Lisa stayed in the nestbox just looking at her babies. She seemed reluctant to leave them to get food. I did not let them have any more babies that year. The next season they had four youngsters but only one of them survived. They managed to rear this one and now seem to know what to do, as since then they have raised several more chicks.

I kept one of their babies, a grey cock split for cinnamon and pied pearl and named him Simon after the cinnamon who died.

In the meantime I had to find a mate for Amy. She had rejected Scott and seemed to fancy Adam but he already had Katy. (It sounds

Above: Cinnamon cock
Right: Cinnamon hen

Above: Four unplucked babies
Below: Five feather-plucked babies

like an episode from one of the soap operas on television). I decided to keep one of Adam's sons, hoping that as he was the image of his dad, Amy might take to him. She did and they have raised lots of chicks. I named her new mate Benjamin.

WORMS

Some breeders will tell you that all birds have worms and must be wormed regularly. My birds do not appear to have worms and I've never wormed any in all the years I've kept them. The only time I have seen a worm was when I first bought Zoe. She came from a pet shop and did not look in such good condition as my birds although I say it myself. It was just after I had paired her off with Timothy, that she passed a worm in her droppings. It was a tape worm and it was dead. I never saw another one and I did not worm her. Within a few weeks she was in as good a condition as all my other birds.

Some worms are not visible to the naked eye but I think that if the birds were plagued by them, the bird's condition would be noticeably poor. Perhaps if the birds are allowed to run around on an earth floor, then there is more likelihood of them picking up worms but my birds have concrete slabs in their flight which are regularly hosed down.

If you suspect that your birds have worms, you should consult your vet and he will advise on what to give and how to administer it to your birds.

THE STRAY BIRD

A friend brought a stray bird to me, a grey split, which had lost a lot of his feathers, presumably from being attacked by wild birds. He was very thin and on the verge of starvation. No one claimed him so I kept him giving him the name Samuel. After I had had him for a little while he took a fancy to one of my white hens, (a daughter of Danny and Emma) and as she also liked him, I decided to keep her and named her Tracy.

She paired off with Samuel but they had problems in their first breeding season. Tracy laid her eggs without any trouble but would not incubate them so Samuel sat day and night. He only left them to get his food and to relieve himself and eventually the eggs hatched. Tracy seemed to think that her job was finished after laying the eggs and Samuel seemed to think that his job was finished after incubating them. Neither of them showed any interest in feeding their offspring and by the time I realised this only one baby was left alive. He also appeared to be dead but I revived him using the gas cooker method.

At about the same time, Zoe and Timothy lost their clutch of eggs (the egg shells were so thin they kept breaking) so I decided to put the revived chick in their nestbox to see if they would foster it. I removed Zoe's nestbox to where she could not see it or what I was doing and threw her cracked eggs away after breaking some shell off one of them. I put pieces of the broken shell back into the nestbox together with the tiny chick and then replaced the nestbox in Zoe's and Timothy's pen. Timothy went straight into the box and had a look at the tiny baby but Zoe would not have anything to do with it. To keep the chick warm I put a heating tray (the sort used in wine making), under the bottom of the nestbox and left it switched on day and night. To stop the box getting too hot, a piece of wood was placed between the box and the heating tray. Over the next few days, Timothy fed the tiny mite now and again but not enough. I tried to help feed it but it would not take anything off me no matter how hard I tried. So I left it hoping that Zoe would perhaps have a change of heart but not she. She completely ignored it but Timothy still carried on feeding it now and then. The baby grew ever so slowly and one morning I found it dead in the nestbox. It was three weeks old but it had the appearance of a twelve day old chick.

When I first acquired Matthew, he was not in the best of conditions. The aviary from which he came was not very special and he did not appear to have any variety in his seed. Once he joined my birds and saw the variety of seeds they had, he just ate and ate. He could not get the food down quick enough. The next morning when I went into the aviary to see to the seed and water, I noticed that he had seeds sticking to his face and crest indicating that he had been vomiting. I watched him for a while and each time he ate anything, he brought it straight back. I gave him some Johnsons Avol (obtainable from pet shops) in his drinking water and this seemed to do the trick and stopped the sickness. A few hours later he passed a lump of undigested seed in his droppings.

One morning, I noticed that Amy was not well, she was not her usual self at all. Her left eye looked flat instead of rounded, it was watering and her eyelids were swollen. Her breathing was heavy and the left side of her cere appeared to be blocked. I thought at first she had a cold and gave her Johnsons Cough and Cold mixture in her drinking water. It was during the summer and the weather was quite warm so I did not think it was necessary to bring her into the house. I kept her penned up in the shelter with her mate but well away from the other birds. A couple of days later she kept rubbing her eye with

Above: Charlie at ten days old
Below: Charlie at three weeks old

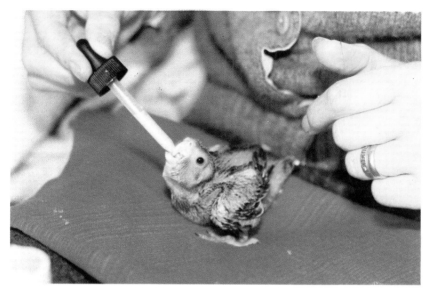

Above: Charlie being fed at two and a half weeks old
Below: Charlie at four weeks. Charlie turned out to be a hen!

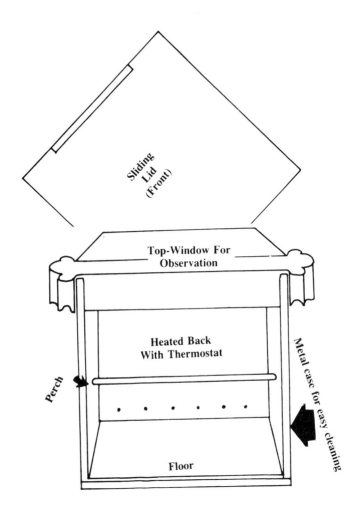

A hospital cage will be useful for dealing with sick birds

her wing as though the eye was itching but she seemed better in herself. However a few days after this, she seemed dull and lifeless and had developed a cough. Her droppings were green diarrhoea so I gave her Terramycin in her drinking water for five days. She gradually improved and after another few days she was better and her old self again. Although Benjamin her mate was penned up with her, he did not become ill himself. He also drank the Terramycin water and I would like to point out that although he was not ill and did not need

Terramycin, it would not do him any harm to drink it.

Later that same summer, Mandy, Jane and one of Jane's daughters all caught colds. They were sneezing and coughing and their eyes looked very watery so I decided to pen them up and gave Terramycin for five days like I did for Amy. This seemed to work for Mandy and Jane so they and their mates, Guy and Matthew, were allowed back into the flight. Jane's daughter, however seemed to have developed bronchitis or asthma. Her breathing was asthmatic which became worse at night. She had a bubbling noise in her chest and she could not whistle, only croak. I brought her into the house to give her extra warmth and gave her Terramycin again for another five days. At the same time I gave her Vick inhalations at night to try and ease her breathing. I covered three sides of the cage with a cloth, placed a container of hot water (to which I had added one teaspoon of Vick) close by the uncovered side of the cage, positioned in such a way that the steam could enter the cage but not burn the bird. There was no improvement after a week so I then tried Harker's Bronchalin Powder concentrate in her drinking water. (This is obtainable from pet shops). This did not help either so I decided to try Aureomycin in her water for seven days. (Aureomycin and Terramycin are anti-biotics and only obtainable from a vet). She seemed to respond to this and there was a definite improvement after the seven days so I continued the treatment for a further five days and she became perfectly well. She no longer got out of breath, the bubbling noise in her chest had disappeared, she whistled instead of croaked and I was able to return her to the aviary, completely cured.

A few weeks later I noticed that Katy had something wrong with her left eye. I thought she had knocked herself somehow because she had been perfectly all right in the morning but in the evening the eye was very watery. The following morning, the eye was swollen shut and was like it for a couple of days. I brought her into the house together with Adam, her mate, and bathed her eye with warm water. I then applied Golden Eye ointment around the eyelids where it was swollen. It was a lot better the next day so I did exactly the same again. I bathed it and applied the ointment. The next day her eye was back to normal so I returned her and Adam back to the aviary.

A couple of days later I noticed that one of the young grey babies had sore eyes, both eyes were bloodshot and were full of matter. The bird looked as if it had three eyelids but what was happening was this: the eyes were discharging and with the eyelids being moist, this kept the matter soft so it moulded to the shape of the eyes. I brought the bird into the house, bathed its eyes each night with warm water and gave Terramycin in its drinking water for five days in case it was an infection. The eyes improved but several other birds in the aviary developed the same problem so I telephoned the vet for his advice. He thought it was a systemic thing and told me it was not necessary to bathe the eyes in this case but to give seven days treatment with Aureomycin. The eye troubles cleared up within a few days after giving the Aureomycin.

ACCIDENTS

Sometimes an accident will occur. One of my baby hens flew into some emulsion paint when I was repainting the shelter. All the birds were outside in the flight at the time but something startled them and they flew around in a panic. The little hen flew straight through the bobhole on to the paintbrush that I was holding and got paint all over her wings and tail. I took her into the house and cleaned her up with a mild hair shampoo.

I gently wet her wings and tail with warm water, put a small amount of neat shampoo on to the painted areas and lathered it up. This was then gently sponged off with warm water. I kept her in the house overnight so she could dry off without catching cold. The next day her feathers had dried out and all the paint had gone so I returned her to the aviary, none the worse for wear.

Talking of shampooing reminds me of an incident concerning Kim. My mother-in-law stayed with us last Christmas and unfortunately became ill with bronchitis. I was washing up when she called to me from the bedroom. (We live in a bungalow by the way). I went to see what she wanted leaving Kim unattended in the kitchen. While I was gone, Kim tried to have a bath in the greasy washing up water. Luckily I heard her splashing and rushed back to rescue her or she might have drowned. She looked a sight. I had to get all the grease off her so first of all I sprayed her with clean *warm* water to which I had added some mild hair shampoo. I then sprayed her with clean *warm* water to get all the soapy lather off and she looked like a drowned rat. I got out my hair dryer and using the warm (not hot) setting, dried her. She loved that part of it so I always use the dryer on her now when she has had a bath.

A friend of mine Mrs Wykes had a young cockatiel off me when he was twelve weeks old. At the time, her husband was ill in hospital and was there for several months. Mrs Wykes spent all her time at the hospital only coming home at mealtimes and to sleep. Monty, the cockatiel was on his own every day the whole of this time. He was not confined to his cage, it was left open all the time so he could please himself what he did. Most of the time he chewed the wall-paper. Understandably he did not tame down until Mrs Wykes lost her husband and spent more time at home with him. After a couple of months, Monty started flying to her and now he sits on her shoulder during the evenings when she watches television. She was very concerned that he still was not talking. I explained that it was probably because she had not spent a lot of time with him when he was younger but not to give up trying. She went on holiday the other week and I looked after Monty for her while she was away. I had him at my house for a fortnight and four days before he went back home, another friend Pat, brought her cockatiel, Jasper to stay for a fortnight while she went on holiday. Now Jasper talks very well and during the four days the two birds were together, Jasper taught Monty to talk but he taught him to say 'hello Jasper' amongst other things. Mrs Wykes was thrilled when she heard him and since she has had him back home and has not mentioned the name Jasper to him, he no longer says it.

I looked after a budgerigar named Bobby for some other friends while they went away but when they brought him to stay he was not at all well. He sat on the floor of his cage with his eyes closed, breathing very heavily. His droppings were just pools of water. I put him in a temperature of 90 degrees F. and gave him Terramycin in his drinking water for five days. I also gave him a drop of the Terramycin water directly into his beak by way of an eye-dropper. After about half an hour he passed a bright green dropping, walked across to his medicated water and had a long drink. He managed to climb onto his perch and throughout the day gradually improved. The next day he started eating and the day after that he seemed perfectly well again.

A neighbour across the road from where I live also had a sick budgie whose symptoms were similar to those of Bobby. Apparently she had placed the bird's cage in front of an open window so I assumed he had been in a draught. My neighbour put on her gas fire and we got the room temperature up to 90 degrees F. I gave the bird the Terramycin treatment the same as Bobby and he responded in exactly the same way. He was perfectly well again within a few days.

A few months ago, I lost Danny, Emma's mate. They had just raised ten chicks, all in one nestbox, eight of their own and two they fostered.

I first noticed something was wrong when I went in to see to the seed and water one morning. It was a few days after the last chick had left the nestbox. I heard noisy asthmatic breathing and found it was Danny. He was on the floor of his pen fighting for breath. I brought him into the house where I could keep an eye on him and treat him as necessary. I brought Emma and their youngest chick in with him and put all three in a large cage. The other chicks were managing to feed themselves so I left them out in the aviary.

I thought Danny had a chest infection. Perhaps he had caught a cold and with feeding all those babies, he was not strong enough to throw it off and it had gone onto his chest, so I gave him Terramycin in the drinking water for five days. I used an infra-red lamp and kept him in a constant temperature of 90 degrees F. During these five days, he ate well, preened his feathers, fed the chick, even did some treading and Emma started laying eggs in the cage. He whistled but sounded hoarse, his feathers were in good condition and his eyes were bright and clear. About every two hours he would go down onto the floor of the cage and gasp for breath for five to ten minutes. When he had these bad bouts I put some menthol crystals in hot water and stood the container by the side of the cage, near where he was sitting, to help ease his breathing.

After the five days' treatment, he did not appear to be getting any better although he did not seem to be any worse, so after consulting the vet I changed the antibiotics from Terramycin to Aureomycin. He then seemed to get progressively worse. He started sneezing twenty to twenty five times in succession, so violently it shook his whole body and he could not keep his feet on the perch. After a sneezing bout he would have a bad breathing spell. He now started going down onto the floor of the cage as soon as he started sneezing as he knew what was coming. He would prop his tail feathers up against the bars of the cage and lie down, his breast feathers resting on the floor. He seemed contented and comfortable in this position.

The sneezing and gasping for breath became more frequent and the bouts lasted longer, every hour for about fifteen to twenty minutes now. I had another word with the vet and was told to stop all antibiotics for about a week and then try again.

Twenty four hours after I stopped the antibiotic treatment, he seemed to be getting better. He tried to whistle to the birds outside and kept preening his feathers over and over again. He then had a very bad turn, he hung onto the bars of the cage with his beak, flapped his wings and cried with pain. His breathing became so bad I thought he was going to die. However, after a while his breathing became easier and he went to sleep on the floor of the cage. About fifteen minutes later, he got up, shook himself and climbed back onto his perch.

The next morning he had a couple of short bouts and then another really bad one and this time he did die. It was terribly upsetting. Emma screamed, went down to the bottom of the cage and tried to revive him. She kept stroking his head feathers with her beak and kept nudging him to try and get him on his feet. It was heartbreaking to see her and I broke down and cried. It was upsetting for me, not only because I had lost a bird and a good one at that, but Danny and Emma were the first breeding pair I owned and I loved them dearly.

I have been advised since that Danny probably had a lung disease and feeding all those babies brought on clinical signs of the disease and although my treatment appeared to help him to a certain extent, he would never have survived. He must have been a strong bird and have had remarkable will-power to have kept bouncing back the way he did after his bad turns.

This last season, Mandy for some unknown reason started plucking her own feathers out, about a week before her eggs were due to hatch. She started at her left ankle and worked all up her leg and the left side of her body. By the time the first egg had hatched, she was completely bald down one side. The only thing I can think of is that it was a case of anxiety because once her eggs had hatched and she had her babies, she stopped doing it and all her feathers have now regrown.

Last year, Adam and Katy had four youngsters, the last one to hatch being a white cock bird who is very small in stature. His tail feathers just would not grow and he looked like a sparrow. Several times the tail feathers started growing but after a couple of inches, they broke off and came out. I could not sell him like this so I kept him. Over the last four months I have been giving him Denes Seaweed tablets crushed and sprinkled onto his seed. I do not know if it is due to these tablets but he started to grow another tail about three weeks ago and this time it looks as if he is going to keep this one. Its about four inches long at the moment and he looks more like a cockatiel now.

I had a problem with Lee, my hand-reared cockatiel. She had been laying eggs consistently since she was 7 months old and by the time she was 14 months, had laid 43. They were not fertile as she did not have a mate and I had been throwing them away as soon as they were laid. It did not seem to bother her that I did this. She used to lay them in the corner of the wall unit behind the ornaments.

Up until then the eggs had been good, but number 43 did not have a shell, just a membrane. Lee had had access to plenty of grit and cuttlefish but it would appear that due to the large amount of eggs she had been laying, her body could no longer produce enough calcium to provide the shell. She was very poorly afterwards, her system was completely drained and she was very weak. She would not eat for a couple of days and could no longer fly. I put her in front of an infra-red lamp for a whole day and Ray told me to give her extra calcium in her water until she improved. At first because she would not drink voluntarily we had to give it to her by way of an eye-dropper. I spent two days trying to get her to eat. I tried hard boiled egg, cheese, biscuits, honey bar as well as millet sprays and her usual seed. She seemed to have difficulty in shelling her usual **seed**, she did not seem to have the strength and kept dropping it so I soaked some in water for twenty four hours to soften it. Gradually she started eating again and slowly regained her strength but it was a full two weeks before she could fly properly again.

I tried to pair her off with three different cock birds but she just was not interested. She thought Roger was her mate. I was told to let her sit on the next lot of eggs she laid. The eggs, not being fertile, would not hatch but Lee might then cease laying for a while.

I tried this but it did not work. She would sit on them for a couple of weeks and then start laying again. I got in touch with a veterinary surgeon who practices homeopathy and he supplied me with some powders to add to her drinking water, one per week for four weeks. This slowed her down but did not stop her. A different powder was given to her for a further four weeks and she stopped laying for two months. She started laying again, had more powders and stopped laying once more. This went on until she was 2 years old, by which time she had laid a grand total of 72 eggs.

Kim, my other pet cockatiel, who is now nine years old, has never laid an egg in her life and doesn't seem to have any desire to do so.

One morning a few weeks ago, I found Susan unwell. She was sitting on the floor in the corner of her pen, breathing very heavily. At the time she had one chick in her nest box, two and a half weeks old, her other eggs not having hatched.

I brought Susan, Nicholas her mate and baby chick complete with nest box into the house and put the whole lot inside a large cage. I gave Susan an eye-dropperful of Terramycin and put some in the drinking water. An infra-red lamp was set up and positioned in such a way that Susan received the benefit of its rays but could move away from it if she wanted to.

As she was too poorly to feed the chick herself, I assumed Nicholas would look after it. However I was wrong. He seemed more worried about his mate than his chick and when I checked on the baby after tea that evening I found it had not been fed. It was so weak from lack of food, it was having convulsions. Every now and again it would hold its head back as if in pain, then roll over on to its side with its legs stretched out straight in front, its claws tightly clenched. It had these convulsions every ten minutes.

First I gave it an eye-dropperful of Terramycin in case he had caught anything off-his mother. I then gave it a drink of honey and water as if for shock. I fed it baby food very slowly with an eye-dropper and as it was too weak to feed voluntarily I trickled the food slowly into its beak and massaged its throat to make it swallow.

After about an hour Roger suggested giving it a few drops of brandy. Now, alcohol should never be given to birds subject to fits. However, as we did not think we had anything to lose we tried it. We had no brandy but gave it an eye-dropperful of whisky and water (a few drops of whisky to an egg cup of water).

Whether it was the whisky or the feeds that I gave little and often I do not know, but the fits gradually stopped over the next hour.

I got up twice during the night to check on the baby and fed it each time. In the morning, it was sitting up and taking notice. His mother regained her health in a couple of days and I put both her and Nicholas back into the outside aviary but I kept the baby indoors and hand reared it. He went from strength to strength and grew into a lovely natured and very tame cock bird.

Getting back to Lee again, one day we noticed she was limping very badly and on closer examination, she had what appeared to be a corn with a scab on it right on the bottom of her foot. My friend Ray told me to bathe the foot in salt water each day and then put the wet foot into some powdered Alum, (obtainable from chemists). This we did and over a period of a couple of weeks, the scab and 'corn' dried up and the limping stopped.

CHAPTER 6

ILLNESSES AND TREATMENTS

A cockatiel is usually a strong, hardy, healthy bird, resistant to illnesses but close confinement and wrong feeding can cause trouble. A healthy bird has a glossy sheen on its feathers and a sleek look to its body. It is alert and bright eyed. If it sits still, looks puffed up and appears drowsy, it may be ill but sometimes a puffed up, sleepy look is perfectly normal. A cockatiel usually sleeps on one leg with the other leg tucked up in his feathers. The best time to check on a bird is in the morning or evening as the bird should be hungry and alert then. During the day they sleep a lot.

SIGNS OF SICKNESS

I can always tell when one of my birds is unwell. The eyes appear to be puffy and half closed instead of shiny and round. Sometimes they have a flat look. The wings are held away from the body, the breathing is heavy and the bird looks thin compared to the others.

Watch the droppings as these are a diary of your bird's health. They are normally black and white and well formed, The black faeces can be affected by the food the bird eats but not many foods affect the white colour of the urine. If the droppings are too watery, bright green or brown, the diet may be wrong or it could be a cold or some other more serious reason.

If it is a cold other symptoms may be present, sneezing, coughing, discharge from the cere and/or watery eyes. The bird must be kept warm, in a temperature of 85 to 90 degrees F. A cockatiel is strong enough to throw off a common cold but if you fail to detect it and do not treat the bird, it could become more serious and you will have to resort to antibiotics. When a cold is first noticed, as I have said before, keep the bird warm and give Johnsons Cough and Cold mixture, (obtainable from most pet shops), in its drinking water. If the cold progresses, then Terramycin or Aureomycin antibiotics must be tried. Your veterinary surgeon will supply this and advise you.

A sick bird will benefit from the heat of an infra-red lamp. As well as giving warmth it also stimulates the circulation of the blood thus activating the production of antibodies. The lamp should be positioned sixteen inches from the cage, in such a way that the light is only on part of the cage so that the bird can move out of the direct rays if it wishes to do so. The lamp should not shine directly onto the seed and water. The temperature should not exceed 90 degrees F. so please keep a close watch on this.

The lamp can be left on for approximately half an hour to an hour and repeated three or four times a day. When the lamp is switched off, keep the temperature in the cage at approximately 85 degrees F.

DIARRHOEA AND CONSITPATION

Diarrhoea is a symptom of many illnesses but is not actually an illness in itself. If your bird suffers from diarrhoea, it again may be his diet. Inflammation of the bowels may occur from feeding stale or mouldy seed. Once the diet has been corrected, the diarrhoea should cease. Greens and fruit cause the droppings to be looser and greener in colour whereas drier foods produce firmer droppings. Diarrhoea can sometimes be cured by putting the bird in a warm temperature, feeding it on a diet of plain canary seed and give boiled water to drink. You can also try sprinkling charcoal onto the seed and give camomile tea to drink instead of the boiled water.

Constipation is usually brought on by feeding a straight seed diet. The birds need and should be given green food. If your bird becomes constipated, try putting a few drops of olive oil into its beak with an eye-dropper or small teaspoon.

Both diarrhoea and constipation can sometimes be cured by giving the bird two tablespoons of Blackstrap Molasses in one quart of boiled water for two days, in place of the normal drinking water. If the bird's condition remains unchanged after five days, repeat the treatment. Do not give this treatment if there is any blood in the diarrhoea or any kind of bleeding from the vent whatsoever.

ANAL PROLAPSE

Sometimes severe constipation or straining to pass an egg can cause the uterus to protrude. This is known as Anal Prolapse. Whatever the causes the uterus must be pushed back gently, using a blunt nosed eyedropper or similar object that has been well greased with vaseline. After the uterus has been replaced, inject some lukewarm saline solution into the vent. Again you can use an eye-dropper. A saline solution is a teaspoon of salt to half a pint of water.

BLEEDING FROM VENT

Bleeding from the vent could have originated in the bowels in which case the blood will be mixed with the faeces. If it originated in the kidneys the urine will be pink or red instead of white. If the bleeding is unmixed with either the faeces or urine, then it most likely originated in the uterus or cloaca. In any case, consult your vet immediately.

Diarrhoea with yellowish to brownish droppings could be due to a liver complaint. If black blood is present, it usually indicates bleeding from the upper digestive tract. Consult your vet immediately.

If the faeces shows whole or undigested seed, this can be a bowel problem, A healthy bird should pass between 40 to sixty droppings in twenty four hours. If the droppings are less than twenty per day it usually indicates a sick bird. If there are no droppings at all, the bird could be very badly constipated, he could have uremic poisoning, (which is described later in the chapter) or he could have a faecal mess sticking to his feathers which is blocking his vent opening. If the bird passes clear or coloured liquid around a dropping, this is not diarrhoea but excess urine which could indicate a kidney disease. Again urgent consultation with a vet is needed.

SAFETY FIRST

When you treat a bird he will most likely struggle and as he may also bite you, it is best to wrap him up in a towel leaving just his face uncovered. If you give him a soluble pill an eye-dropper is probably the easiest way. If you have to give him a pill that will not dissolve in water, you must cut it up very small. You can wet your fingers and rub the sharp edges of the pill so as to smooth them and then gently push the pieces of pill down the birds throat with a toothpick or similar object. A piece of cotton can be wrapped around the toothpick so that it will not hurt the birds throat when you use it. Be very careful that you do not push the pill down the windpipe instead of the throat.

BALD PATCHES

White cockatiels have a tendency to baldness on the top of their heads behind the crest. This bald patch varies in size from bird to bird but whether the patch is large or small, it is nothing to worry about. Sometimes it is hereditary and nothing can be done. However, baldness can occur when chicks are feather-plucked in the nestbox and the parent birds damage the feather follicles. They sometimes grow again but it can take a long time for the pin feathers to grow through the toughened skin. I have recently read an article in a health magazine that states, if a powder called Selenium, obtainable from a homeopathic vet, is given in the bird's drinking water and Denes Skin Balm is applied to the bald patches, it will help new feathers to grow. The cream or balm is supposed to stimulate new skin production by bringing the blood to the outer skin layer, causing the old skin to flake off and new feather follicles to grow with the new skin. Selenium is a source of vitamin E. I have also been advised that if olive oil is rubbed repeatedly onto the bald patches, this will help feathers to start growing again. This is something I have yet to try.

At the present time I have a dozen pair of cockatiels and of these I have three pairs in which the cock bird plucks his hen around the head and neck and three pairs in which the cock bird is slightly plucked on the head by the hen. Five of the twelve pairs feather-pluck their chicks and two of these pluck them so badly they look like chickens ready for the oven when they come out of the nestbox. The other three pairs just pluck their babies around the neck and head so they resemble vultures.

If baldness is due to the destruction of the feathers caused by the birds fighting etc, it is best to let nature take its course. The wing and tail feathers, upon which the bird's life depends, are replaced whenever they are lost, but the body feathers are not usually replaced until the bird has its next moult. However, chicks that have been feather-plucked in the nestbox will grow new feathers at once unless, as I previously stated, the follicles have been damaged. I have found with my birds that if the chicks have been feather-plucked on the head when in the nestbox and then after these feathers have regrown, the parents pluck them out again for a second time, they do not grow for a third time until the chick has its first moult.

BROKEN FEATHERS

Broken and bleeding feathers are caused by the birds banging themselves against the sides of their cages, perches or wires in the flight. If the feather is broken close to the blood supply it will bleed. If the bleeding is excessive you will have to help or the bird could bleed to death. Get someone to hold the bird in a towel so that you can hold out the injured wing with one hand, grasp the damaged feather with the other hand and pull it out. The bleeding should now stop and a new feather grow within a few weeks.

OVERGROWN BEAK OR CLAWS

Sometimes the beak and claws get overgrown and need trimming. I have already explained in Chapter 1 how these problems can be dealt with but there is one thing I would like to mention here and that is, please do not buy the sandpaper covers that fit over a bird's perch in the belief that they will keep the claws filed down. Maybe they will, but think about it. How would you like to stand with bare feet on sandpaper for most of your lifetime. The birds feet will get very sore and he will be most uncomfortable and unhappy.

SORE FEET

Talking of sore feet, if a bird has injured its foot and it is an open wound, wrap the patient in a towel and hold the foot in a cup of *warm* water containing a few drops of Amplexol. If he has sprained or twisted his foot and it is just swollen and painful to walk on, you can bathe it daily with *warm* water to which a few drops of witch hazel have been added. Amplexol is obtainable from most pet shops and the witch hazel from chemists.

BROKEN LIMBS

If a bird breaks either a leg or a wing keep him quiet and remove all his perches for the time being to discourage him from climbing. Put all food and water in open dishes and place them within easy reach of the patient. Feed him a good diet and give him a tonic in his drinking water such as Johnsons cage bird tonic. The bird will favour his broken leg or wing and not use it. It should heal in about ten days.

If the wing hangs in a graceful droop as if the bird is holding it naturally, then leave well alone but if it hangs abnormally, then it must be folded back against the bird's side in as natural a position as possible. It should be held in place by a strip of adhesive tape wrapped around the body leaving the other wing free. If in any doubt consult the vet.

Leg fractures need to be seen by a vet as not all of them can be set.

When a bird injuries itself, it may suffer from shock. If this happens, he stops moving, his eyes cannot focus and his breathing becomes shallow. Warmth is essential and he must be kept quiet.

MITES

Do not think that your bird will never get mites. Red mites are very tiny, the size of a pin head. They feed on the bird's blood at night and can be the cause of the hen leaving the nestbox. During the daytime they hide away in cracks or crevices under roosts etc but can be seen by torchlight at night on perches in dark rooms. Red mites weaken the birds making them anaemic, dull and droopy with little or no appetite. Sprays can be bought from pet shops.

SCALY FACE

Another tiny mite can cause a condition known as scaly face and legs. It is very contagious so the infected bird must be isolated and the cage and perches disinfected. Scabs appear around the beak and cere and on the legs and feet of the bird.

These can be treated with Johnsons Scaly Leg remedy (obtainable from pet shops) but as an alternative, the affected areas can be soaked with olive oil. If using the oil, repeat the application again three days later and the scabs should then be removed very carefully with tweezers.

CONJUNCTIVITIS

Another contagious ailment is conjunctivitis and this can be caused by a scratch, draught or infection. If it is neglected, the bird could go blind. You must isolate the bird, bathe the eyes regularly and apply either Golden Eye ointment to the eyelids or Chloromycetin eye ointment. Golden Eye ointment is obtainable from the chemist and Chloromycetin from a vet. I have recently been told by a chemist that Golden Eye ointment has been taken off the market.

SWELLING

Sometimes a bird develops a small angry-looking swelling which is usually caused by an injury from sharp wire etc. This could be an abscess in which case it can be treated with Amplexol. The Amplexol is diluted in warm water and the swelling bathed with this solution. Do not have the water too hot, it should just be comfortable for the bird. If this does not do the trick consult the vet. Amplexol is obtainable from pet shops.

OIL GLAND INFLAMMATION

A bird has an oil gland which is found at the base of its tail on the upper side. The purpose of this gland is to secrete oil which the bird uses to preen its feathers. If the gland opening becomes blocked, inflammation is set up by a backlog of oil. When this happens, the swelling resembles a tumour and the backlog of oil must be removed. You can do this with a matchstick or toothpick, applying gentle pressure until the gland is clear. If it does not squeeze out easily or there is any bleeding, consult the vet as the swelling may be a tumour after all and not a blockage.

DIGESTION PROBLEMS

Sometimes a bird's crop becomes sour through digestive upsets. The bird retches and vomits seed and liquid which has a sour smell. Dissolve a teaspoon of bicarbonate of soda in a quart of water and give this to the bird instead of its normal drinking water. This should sweeten the crop in a few days. You can also try a teaspoon of Enos salts to a quart of water. If there is no improvement, consult the vet as sour crop can be caused by a mould.

A parent bird can sometimes fill a baby bird's crop so full of seeds it cannot digest them. When this happens the crop appears hard and the chick is uncomfortable so the crop must be washed out. Give the chick two or three dropperfulls of warm water to which a pinch of bicarbonate of soda has been added, (a saltspoon of bicarbonate of soda to one fluid ounce of *warm* water). Massage the crop until the seed loosens and then by holding the bird's head down, empty its crop by massaging it towards the mouth. This should be repeated until the crop is completely cleaned out.

Before leaving the chick to rest, give him a dropperful of water to drink, this time a half a teaspoon of bicarbonate of soda to a cup of water.

SWEATING

One of the causes of chicks dying in the nestbox between the sixth and tenth day of hatching is sweating or nestling diarrhoea. This is caused by stale or mouldy food. The chicks develop a thin watery diarrhoea which fouls the nest and because of the dampness of the nestbox, the breast feathers of the hen become matted. She also has a grey, stringish diarrhoea. If noticed in time, clean out the nestbox but put the chicks in a safe and warm place while you do it.

When the nestbox is completely clean and dry you can replace the chicks. I do not advise you to remove the chicks to another nestbox instead of cleaning the original one. Remember the case of Jane in Chapter 5.

GASTRO-ENTERITIS

Inflammation of the intestines or gastro-enteritis is either caused by bad food or an infection. The bird will be in pain, its body tense and swollen and its feathers all fluffed up. It will have an excessive thirst and will sometimes be retching. The droppings will be thin, slimy, green or red and the bird's vent will be stained and dirty. The patient should be isolated and put in a temperature of 80 to 85 degrees F. Clean the bird's vent with warm diluted Amplexol and using either the same solution or other disinfectant, clean the cage and perches. Make sure that all food and water is fresh and clean. Give Terramycin in the drinking water for a period of five days. Your vet will advise you on the dosage.

CHILLS

If a bird gets chilled or is in a draught, his body temperature drops and this can cause the urine to crystallise in his little uriniferous tubes, blocking them. The result is uremic poisoning. The bird will be puffed up like a ball, seeming cold and shivery and wants to sleep all the time. He eats and drinks very little and becomes weaker by the minute. He will stand first on one leg and then on two until he finally becomes so weak he can no longer grasp his perch. He will then go down onto the floor of the cage and as the illness progresses, his breathing becomes more rapid and shallow and there are no droppings. He will just sit there until he falls over dead. If not caught in time, the bird can die within twenty four hours from the start of the illness. Warmth is essential so place him in a hospital cage in a temperature of, 80 to 85 degrees F. If caught in time, a bird can recover without any other treatment within a few hours.

If your bird catches cold and this cold is neglected, it can turn to bronchitis. The bird will huddle on its perch with ruffled feathers. He will have a dry cough, will gasp for breath and be wheezy. Put his cage in a temperature of 75 to 80 degrees F. and give medicated inhalations at night.

To do this, cover the cage on three sides with a cloth, add a few drops of Friars Balsam or Eucalyptus Oil or a teaspoon of Vick to a bowl of steaming hot water. Place the bowl close to the uncovered side of the cage so that the steam can enter. Never place the bowl inside the cage, the bird could get burnt. Keep the bird warm afterwards. Also give Aureomycin in his drinking water for five to six days and if there is no improvement, consult the vet.

OTHER DISEASES

The same medicated treatment can also be tried for aspergillosis which is caused by a fungus or mould from food or dust. The bird is dull and lifeless with ruffled feathers, it is wheezy, gasping for breath and sometimes has a discharge from its nostrils or cere. It stands with both feet on the ground or floor of its cage with its eyes closed. Consult a vet immediately.

A vet should also be consulted immediately psittacosis or parrot fever is suspected. Do not handle either the bird or its cage as psittacosis is caused by a virus, the illness resembling pneumonia and can be passed to humans. The bird is very ill and weak with dropping wings. It has loose, green diarrhoea tinged with blood, it shivers and has fits and convulsions leading to death. Psittacosis today is extremely rare.

If all efforts to cure a sick bird fail, the bird is in pain and obviously going to die, it is better to put it painlessly to sleep than to prolong its suffering. The best method I know is to place the bird in a paper bag and hold the end of the bag around a car exhaust. It takes less than a minute for the carbon monoxide to have done its painless work. The bird just goes into everlasting sleep. Alternatively, you can take the bird to a vet for him to put it down, but please never drown it or wring its neck.

CASES

A workmate of mine lost one of her pet cockatiels a few days ago. It seemed perfectly all right during the day, then all of a sudden in the evening it began to swell up like a balloon. The swelling started around the neck and then the face and finally the whole body. The bird looked grotesque, its movements were very awkward and it could not grip its perch. It sat on the floor of the cage rocking back and forth and the following morning it was dead. The only thing I can think of is that it was an air tube or air sac rupture and the bird's heart gave out due to shock or pressure on the heart. This rupture occurs either as a latter stage of an infectious disease, being incorrectly cared for, i.e. poor diet, or it could be due to an injury. As far as my friend's bird was concerned, its diet was correct in every way and I do not think it had an infectious disease as she had two birds in the same cage and the other one is still perfectly all right. As far as she was aware the bird had not injured itself but it was possible because whenever she let it out of its cage, it flew around the room like a mad thing and occasionally bumped itself. Whatever the cause, the skin has to be punctured and the air drawn off. If the cause is an infectious disease, the bird would have shown other symptoms prior to the rupture and the illness will have to be diagnosed and treated. If the cause is a poor diet, this can easily be corrected, making sure that the bird has plenty of green food and Vitamin D. If the cause is an injury, this again will have to be diagnosed and treated. If your bird swells up in this way, consult the vet immediately.

Now a final word about Lee and sadly it is a final word as she is no longer with us. She died on 11th August 1989, aged 2 years 3 months. It was sudden and a great shock. She seemed perfectly all right at dinnertime when I put her in her cage and left her to go to work at twelve o'clock. She had been flying around, playing and eating as normal during the morning but when Roger came home at five o'clock she was sitting on the floor of her cage. She tried to whistle to him like she usually does but she was having difficulty in breathing and there were terrible noises in her chest. He picked her up and she put her head down to be stroked. He stoked her, she gave a shudder and died in his hands. It was as if she had waited for him to come home. When he laid her down on the floor of her cage, blood came out of her mouth. The vet was of the opinion she had had a massive haemhorrage, possibly a respiratory haemhorrage which affected her heart and there was nothing we could have done. He said she would have died very quickly. Both Roger and I miss her dreadfully. We loved her so much.

CHAPTER 7

CONCLUSIONS

I would like to emphasise that this book is based on experiences with my cockatiels. Other people may experience different problems but if this book has helped in any way, then it will all have been worth while.

I would like to bring to your attention a few more facts that have not previously been mentioned and to recap on several points that I think are important.

FIRST SIGNS OF SICKNESS

If housed with other birds, the sick one may be sitting alone on the floor and not on a perch with the others. He may be dull and sleepy, have no appetite, have excessive thirst, diarrhoea may be present or he may be constipated. He may have a cough, be wheezy, be huddled on his perch, shivering, with both feet clutching the perch. His eyes may be dull, puffy or watery and his feathers may be untidy. His breathing may be heavy and his feathers all puffed out. Has he a dirty vent or a discoloured face or cere? Is he losing weight (going light – thin breastbone)? Has he any lumps or sores?

Immediate warmth of 80 to 90 degrees F. and treatment can prevent serious illness. If the bird is in shock, handle it as little as possible. If the sick bird is with other birds, isolate the patient so if any disease is present it cannot spread. If possible, put its mate with it or within sight and sound of it so it does not fret. A sick bird should be put in a hospital cage equipped with a heating lamp and a thermometer. A thermometer is very useful as it ensures that the temperature is gradually increased to 80 to 90 degrees F. A bird stands a good chance of recovery provided it is kept warm and continues to eat.

HOSPITAL CAGES

If you do not have a hospital cage put the bird in a spare room where you can *gradually* bring the room temperature up to the required degrees F. For extra warmth, you can cover the cage with a cloth leaving the front uncovered. You could also use an infra-red lamp as described in a previous chapter. Once the bird has recovered, you can gradually reduce the temperature of the room back down to what the bird is accustomed to. If the temperature drops too quickly, the bird could catch a chill. I would like to point out that if a sick bird is brought into the house during the winter and given extra warmth, it should not be put back into the aviary as soon as it is well, but kept indoors until the warmer weather, otherwise the bird will catch cold.

Never put a bird in front of a direct source of heat, i.e. a gas fire, as a bird has hollow bones that are filled with air and sudden heat causes the air to expand causing the bird pain and discomfort and in most cases, death.

Unless it is too ill to do so, a sick bird drinks frequently and will usually take medicine in its drinking water. If not, use an eye-dropper and give the drops slowly onto the *back of the tongue*, one drop at a time. If more is given you may choke the bird. Do not give treatments by mouth if the bird is prone to fits.

INJURIES

If a bird is injured and the wound is a minor one, add a few drops of Amplexol to a little hot water and bathe the wound each day using cotton wool. Make sure that the water is not too hot. Do not use ointments and do not cover body wounds with bandages or other dressings. Antibiotics should only be used for deep and infected wounds.

SOAKED SEEDS

A sick bird is best fed on soaked seeds. These seeds are easier for the bird to digest and less difficult to crack. If the bird will not eat you can try giving honey water (half honey and half water) and give directly into the mouth with an eye-dropper. Do not give more than a couple of drops at a time in case the liquid goes down into the lungs and chokes the bird.

OTHER HINTS

1   A sick bird, taken to the vet, must be kept warm. Get the car warm first and cover the cage with a cloth. Try and keep the bird in an even temperature.

2   When a bird moults it is generally off colour as replacing its body feathers saps its strength. Give it a tonic in its drinking water. Older birds sometimes get weak and sickly and if this happens, an infra-red lamp should be used, two or three times a day, half an hour at a time. Also give the bird a tonic.

3   Watch out for open doors and windows. Don't think that because you have venetian blinds at the window, your bird cannot get out. Cockatiels can climb up and down venetian blinds and get through them.

4   Beware of sudden changes in room temperature. Cockatiels are very sensitive to draughts. Neither should they be in direct sun or in an overheated room, they could suffer from sun or heatstroke and have even been known to die.

5   They are nosy birds and like to get inside cupboards and drawers so be careful you do not shut your bird up in one. They can also slip down inside empty vases and get stuck so watch out for this. Never let your bird loose in the kitchen. He could get scolded, burnt or drowned.

6   Do not use air sprays to freshen the room, flysprays or plant insecticides where there is a cockatiel as these are all poisonous to the bird.

7   A few more words about worms. I can remember reading some-where that the Caribbean Indians used to cure their pet parrots of worms by giving them the milk (squeezed out of the meat) of a coconut to drink. The birds usually passed the worms within a week. I do not know if it really works as I have never had cause to try it. You could also try Denes Garlic Tablets.

HERBAL REMEDIES

I am a great believer in Denes Herbal products for pets and have tried Greenleaf, Garlic and Seaweed on my birds. The Greenleaf tablets contain chlorophyll, ferrous sulphate and nettle powder. They cleanse acidity from the system and are for skin complaints, rheuma-tism, acid conditions and persistent scratching. I tried Greenleaf on Timothy for rheumatism in his leg and after three months treatment his leg got better. The Garlic tablets contain garlic and garlic oil, nothing else. Garlic is nature's strongest internal disinfectant and the tablets are used for worms, diarrhoea, coughs and catarrh. I gave Guy some for persistent diarrhoea and the tablets cleared it up in a couple of weeks. The Seaweed tablets are just seaweed and they are used for poor or dull coats, feather growth and overweight problems. I give them to my birds to keep their feathers in good condition. I crush all tablets up and sprinkle them over the seed. Denes Herbal tablets are obtainable from some pet shops and most health stores.

CATCHING UP

If you need to catch hold of a bird for any reason, reach for it in the correct manner. Your right hand should be placed against its breast and with your left hand reach down over its head. The head should rest between your thumb and first finger, with the other fingers around its tummy. *Do not squeeze its chest or abdomen.* If it is not tame enough to be caught easily during the day you could always wait until it is dark and then try and catch hold of it.

A cockatiel's cage should be large enough for the bird to stand up straight, extend its wings and stretch without any part of its body touching the cage. Make sure that the bars are not too wide apart, about three quarters of an inch is ideal, as you do not want the bird to get its head through. As I mentioned before, the cage door if hinged on the bottom can be fastened open and in this way becomes a landing stage. Roger used a piece of a broom handle to prop the door open. He cut grooves in each end of the wood so it slotted onto the wire in the same way that the perches do. A piece of dowelling would also do the trick.

MORE HINTS

Do not buy ornamental cages. They may look pretty but are not usually very practical. If you go to a private dealer for your bird, buy the cage first and take it with you when you fetch the bird but make sure it is a suitable cage for a cockatiel. If it is not suitable, a good breeder will make you change it before parting with any of his birds. Before I let mine go as pets I like to see the cage first. I like to make sure that they will be happy and comfortable in their new homes. After all, they will have to spend a lot of time in them.

Be sure that you feed the correct food for a cockatiel and make sure that all foods (seeds, greens and fruit) and water are fresh and greens and fruit are not fed straight from the fridge. Do not feed greens and grasses picked from roadsides as the poisonous exhaust fumes from vehicles get onto the plants and cannot be washed off properly. They can be fatal to birds.

There are a couple of ways to test if seeds are fresh. One, using your thumb press a small seed onto a sheet of paper and a small circle of oil should be left on the paper. Two, if the seed is planted in soil or soaked in water, it should sprout. These sprouts can be given to your bird and are very good for him. If the seed when planted or soaked does not sprout, then it is not good seed and should not be given to your bird.

Soak some seeds in one inch of water for about twenty four hours. Then rinse them well with lukewarm water and if left covered (not airtight) for another twenty four hours, the seed should have sprouted. Soaked seed is also beneficial and the method is the same as above only the seeds are ready to be fed to the birds after they have been rinsed and not left for a further twenty four hours. Both sprouted and soaked seed spoil quickly so if they are fed to your birds in the morning, any remaining should be removed in the late afternoon and thrown away.

Even the cleanest seed can get moth larvae or weevils in it and if this does happen, it can be got rid of by baking the seed in the oven for about a quarter of an hour.

If you have a heated shelter and want to start breeding with your birds early in the year, you must make sure that they get a minimum of twelve hours of light, in which to feed their babies. This can be achieved by installing a dimmerlight in the shelter connected to a time switch. There are quite a few models available on the market at various prices.

Don't throw eggs away too soon. Leave at least twenty eight days as some birds do not start sitting straight away.

I read an article the other week how some researchers in America had come up with a theory, that the cause of a lot of baby cockatiels dying in the nestbox is due to a crop mould and not starvation by the parent birds as previously thought. The mould causes sore mouths and because of this the youngsters refuse to take food off their parents and therefore starve to death. The article went on to say that by administering Vitamin A to the parent's diet prior to the eggs hatching, this problem is overcome. I always give my birds plenty of vitamins all the year round.

Some cockatiels pick up their first words in a few weeks but others do take longer so do not be disheartened if your pet does not start talking as soon as you would like him to. Pick out one word to start with, his name for instance, and keep repeating it over and over again. Once he has learnt to say this, go on to another word. You will find that once your bird says its first word, it will pick up others much more quickly. As I have mentioned before, try recording your voice on tape and play the tape over and over again to your bird.

One of the questions I get asked a lot is do cockatiels make much noise. A single pet cock bird can be noisy at times. Most of the time he will whistle and talk but occasionally he will scream if something upsets him. I find hens are much quieter companions. If you want to keep cockatiels in an outside aviary, a few of them should not annoy your neighbours. However, they can be fairly noisy first thing in the morning and again in the evening before they go to bed but during the day they are usually quiet. They preen and sleep most of the time. I have twelve pairs and my neighbours do not mind them, or so they say. Occasionally something will upset the birds, a cat wandering into the garden, a magpie or crow hovering overhead or a stranger is about. My birds always let me know when anyone strange comes to the house, in that respect they are as good as any dog.

If your pet bird feather-plucks himself, it could be because he has a skin disorder, he is bored, lonely or grieving over a lost mate. Sometimes when a bird changes hands, it will pine for its previous owner. Try giving it hard boiled egg, fresh branches to chew, a new mate or a mirror, and spend more time with the bird. Cockatiels love company and want to be with their owners if they do not have a mate or another bird for company. If you can't keep the cage in the room where you spend most of your time, please do not keep a lone cockatiel for a pet.

If you already own a cockatiel and want to buy another one as a companion for it, please do not put the new bird directly into your pet bird's cage. The cage is its own territory and your first pet will feel threatened until it gets to know the newcomer. The two birds should be allowed to gradually get to know one another. Put the new bird in a separate cage for the time being and site it where the two birds can see one another. Let them out of their cages to have a fly round the room, alternately at first and then after a few days, let them out together. When you see the birds entering each others cages and there is no squabbling, you can then leave the two birds in one cage.

Never go out shopping etc and leave your bird loose in the room. He could get caught in the curtains and injure himself or slip down behind wall units or a radiator and get trapped. If you are at home and he gets caught anywhere, you will hear him screaming and be able to go to his aid. As cockatiels are nosy, inquisitive birds, always shut them in their cages before going out of the house.

If you give your cockatiel plenty of love and attention, it will reward you by returning that affection. Never tease the bird as this can turn him from a friendly lovable bird into a spiteful one. You will find that he likes to be stroked on the head, if not with your finger then gently with your nose and will spend hours sitting on your shoulder or your lap. He will want to spend more and more time with you and less time shut up in his cage. Both hens and cock birds make excellent pets. Provided he or she has a well balanced diet, clean food and water, clean living quarters, plenty of exercise and you give him or her lots of attention, you will have an affectionate and devoted little friend for a number of years.

INDEX